THE

Passionate

CHURCH

LIFESHAPES
The Language of Leadership

THE
Passionate
CHURCH

MIKE BREEN AND WALT KALLESTAD

Building the New Generation of Believers

COOK COMMUNICATIONS MINISTRIES
Colorado Springs, Colorado • Paris, Ontario
KINGSWAY COMMUNICATIONS, LTD
Eastbourne, England

NexGen® is an imprint of

Cook Communications Ministries, Colorado Springs, CO 80918

Cook Communications, Paris, Ontario

Kingsway Communications, Eastbourne, England

THE PASSIONATE CHURCH

© Copyright 2005 by Mike Breen and Walt Kallestad

First printing 2004

Printed in Canada

3 4 5 6 7 8 9 10 Printing/Year 09 08 07 06 05

Cover Design: Bill Chiaravalle, BrandNavigation, LLC
Cover Photo: Photodisc, Pat Powers and Cherryl Schafer

Mike Breen is the creator and developer of the LifeShapes material (formerly called LifeSkills) and the eight (8) shapes as a memorable method of discipleship.

ISBN: 0-78144-227-3

To The Order of Mission
and the many team members who have contributed
to LifeShapes throughout the years

—MIKE

To my kids,
Patrick, Shannon, Shawn-Marie, and Brian,
who pressed me to my new place of life and ministry

—WALT

ACKNOWLEDGMENTS

Although many have added to this process we now call LifeShapes, some deserve a special mention: Mike Williams from Cranmer Hall Durham, who introduced me to my first "learning loop"; Malcolm Wylie, who shared with me a "leadership square" in Cambridge (see chapters 13 and 14); Martin Lee, who helped with the development of Up, In, Out; and Bob and Mary Hopkins, who shared with me George Pattison's triangle as a way of organizing these three dimensions.

In Sheffield, many helped and contributed, but Paul Richards, Paddy Mallon, Mal Calladine, Arlene Moore, Nigel Mallon, and Paul Maconochie were especially helpful. It has been enormous fun over the years learning what LifeShapes is all about . . . who knows how many hours we have spent together extrovertly processing over coffee. Now in the U.S.A., my good friend Walt Kallestad has been an invaluable aid and ally to all that LifeShapes has become. I acknowledge you all and give thanks to God for all he has taught me through you. Finally, a special thanks to Janet Lee and Jeff Dunn and the team at Cook Communications Ministries for their amazing commitment to this project. I can't thank you enough.

MIKE BREEN

ACKNOWLEDGMENTS

A very special thanks to: my "buddy" Mike Breen and The Order of Mission; Eddie Gibbs; Ryan Boldger; Brian McClaren; Dan Kimball; Mike Erre; the Cook Team—Jeff Dunn, Janet Lee, Dick Frieg; Len Sweet; Steve and Sue Perry; . . . and to every kingdom worker who is living through seismic transition for the sake of unstoppable transformation of human hearts.

Walt Kallestad

CONTENTS

Meet the Authors   13

Introduction   15

1. What's Our Job?   21

2. The Shapes of Discipleship   27

3. It's About Time   35

4. A Lifestyle of Learning   41

5. Life Is Like a Slinky   47

6. Living in Rhythm with Life   59

7. Working from Rest   67

8. Your Personal Style of Rest   73

9. Jesus and the Balanced Life   81

10. What's Up?   89

11. Balancing Our In Relationships   95

12. Balance Our Out Reach   101

13. Defining the Priorities of Life   109

14. The Language of Leadership   121

15. Who Does Your Church Belong To?   133

16. The Fivefold Foundation for Ministry   141

17. Discerning Your Core Calling   149

18. Living a Life of Prayer   157

19. Practicing the Six Principles of Prayer   167

20. Practicing the Principles of a Vital Life   175

21. Signs of Life   185

22. Living a Mission-Minded Life   197

23. Empowering Evangelism   203

24. Conclusion   215

Appendix   219

Endnotes   227

A Passionate Life (Sample Chapter)   229

MEET THE AUTHORS

Pastor Walt Kallestad had spent more than twenty years building Community Church of Joy in Phoenix, Arizona, into a seeker-friendly assembly of 12,000 when his heart nearly failed him. In January 2002 Walt suffered a major heart attack; only six-way bypass surgery and the grace of God kept him from going home to heaven at a relatively young age.

The physical trauma forced Walt to take a year-long sabbatical. During this time he did some serious evaluation of the state of his church and the direction in which it was moving—and whether he should continue leading it. He sought counsel from pastors across the country. Finally, a trusted friend gently forced Walt to acknowledge that his huge flock had lost its community, its authenticity—its passion. Besides, who would want to take on the mammoth responsibilities of running a megachurch when he could walk on the cutting edge of modern ministry? And where did that leave Community Church of Joy? Walt's search moved in a new direction: overseas.

Pastor Mike Breen, Rector and team leader of St. Thomas Church (an Anglican and Baptist Church) in Sheffield, England, had grown one of the largest churches in England with more than two thousand attending weekly worship, 70 percent of which are under the age of 35.

One of Walt's peers suggested he visit St. Thomas Church in Sheffield, England. One visit to St. Thomas left Walt amazed at the depth of spiritual growth and authentic community he sensed among the people. One conversation with Mike Breen left him intrigued with a new concept and approach to teaching and discipleship: LifeShapes.

Mike had spent the better part of a decade developing this visually oriented teaching tool. LifeShapes had certainly proved its effectiveness among the members of this largely twenty- and thirty-something congregation. It was helping them not only to understand biblical principles on a deeper level, but also to apply those principles to their lives. St. Thomas Church had become a church passionate to know Christ and to make him known.

Mike and Walt made a connection in that conversation. It proved to be a life-changing moment . . . a *kairos* moment. God stepped into the circumstances of these two men and pulled the loose ends of their worlds together. Creator of LifeShapes, Mike has recently moved to the U.S. to teach at Fuller Theological Seminary in Pasadena, CA, serve on the staff of Walt's church in Glendale, AZ, and travel the country speaking on LifeShapes. Now, as a staff member of Community Church of Joy, Mike is teaching the principles of LifeShapes and helping the church to once again reflect the foundation of its name: *community*.

INTRODUCTION

*F*ebruary 3, 1931, began as a quiet Tuesday morning in the beautiful coastal region of Hawkes Bay in New Zealand. The residents of Napier and Hastings, the two main towns in that area, went about their business as they had for decades. Customers were keeping the banks busy. Shops were filled with merchandise and eager buyers. Restaurants were clearing away the last of the breakfast dishes and preparing for the lunch crowd. Those on holiday made plans to go to the beach. In other words, life was going on as it had always been and probably would always be as the sun rose over these idyllic villages.

Then, at 10:46 in the morning, everything changed. An earthquake struck. In less than three minutes, seismic forces reaching 7.9 on the Richter scale destroyed most of the buildings in both towns, killing hundreds of people. Those structures not flattened by the quake were destroyed in the subsequent fire that swept through the ruins.

Once the smoke and dust cleared, the residents of Napier and Hastings were met with a great surprise. The shattered landscape bore little resemblance to the terrain they had known so well. Landmarks such as Napier Bluff Hill, a popular tourist destination, had been torn from the coast and tossed into the sea. What had once been flat ground was now a series of hills. Where there had been valleys, there was now level ground. Most shocking of all was the discovery that the water in Ahuriri Lagoon had somehow been swallowed up, leaving nine thousand acres of dry ground.

When the residents of Hawkes Bay set about rebuilding their town, they faced a dilemma. The extent to which the earthquake had changed their environment was astonishing. Their maps of the region no longer applied; those maps showed roads running along land that no longer existed. And they did not show the new land heaved up by the earthquake.

Eventually the towns of Napier and Hastings were successfully rebuilt in the art deco style of the time (and to this day remain among the best examples of period architecture in the world) because those who directed the rebuilding threw out their maps and instead relied on a compass. When the landscape changes, maps are useless, but the compass is still trustworthy.

SOCIAL QUAKES AND CULTURAL SHIFTS

Throughout history, seismic cultural quakes have affected our social landscape and with it the context of the church. Jesus was born in the midst of economic and political turmoil in the Roman-controlled territory of Israel. Emperor Caesar Augustus ordered a census of his kingdom in order to count the population and set tax rates. Every fourteen years a regular census was taken, with additional counts taken periodically. But this was an unusual census, as everyone was ordered to return to his ancestral home. Almost everyone in the empire could be considered a refugee without a permanent home; basically, the whole empire was on the move. The Jewish Pharisees, who thrived on controlling situations and circumstances with their laws and traditions, saw their world in upheaval.

Jesus was born in the midst of that upheaval. During his entire life on earth, the social and religious boundaries continued to shift. Just a few decades after his crucifixion and resurrection, the situation came to a head as the Romans leveled the Jewish temple and dismantled the Jewish government.

Four hundred years later, another quake occurred. The eleven-centuries-old Roman Empire, weakened from within by political and spiritual struggles, fell. Vandals who crossed the frozen Rhine in 406 AD seeking better lands, attacked—and conquered. The humiliated Romans looked for a place to fix blame for this catastrophe. They found Christians to be an easy target. The

> IN THE MIDST OF CHAOS AND CONFUSION, IT WAS THE CHURCH THAT LED THE WAY.

ancient gods, they determined, had become angry that so many people were converting to Christianity. Augustine, then bishop of Hippo in Roman Africa, argued that the Christians were not at fault; pagan behavior had hastened Rome's fall. Augustine's writings, most notably *City of God*, gave a compass reading that the church followed for the next one thousand years. In the midst of chaos and confusion, it was the church that led the way.

The next seismic shift occurred during the Renaissance. The invention of the printing press allowed the mass production and distribution of the written word, including Scripture. It changed forever how people think and learn. With access to the Bible now freed from tight control by the church, its truths became widely known, including the idea that salvation was by grace through faith alone. Thus the Reformation was ushered in, creating yet another upside-down event for the church. At the same time, a new science-based worldview emerged, introducing a cultural elite, including Galileo, Newton, Bacon, and Copernicus. Market capitalism replaced feudalism, and that—combined with the development of modern weaponry (gunpowder and long guns)—brought about the rise of the nation-state. Once again, old maps were tossed aside as no longer useful.

TODAY'S CULTURAL UPHEAVAL

We are now going through a similar shaking—a cultural earthquake. Our reference points have changed; our familiar social landscape is now so altered that many find it difficult to navigate through life. The global change seen most clearly in the West has resulted in a postindustrial, high-tech society, and a whole new way of thinking. In the last few years, this new landscape has come to be described as postmodernism. The phenomenal rate of change at the social and political levels of society has been breathtaking and appears to be accelerating. Never before has a society become so permissive, so dislocated and disjointed, so incapable of maintaining order, stability, and balance.

Alongside the social upheaval, amazing technological advances have gathered momentum at an incredible pace. We are trying to understand a world that no longer submits to the powers of familiar reason and logic. This profoundly affects the way that we communicate and, because of this, the way that we form community. With the development of this new worldview, a whole new context for doing church has emerged.

The church has not adapted well to these changes. The measurable decline in church attendance of the postmodern generation, comprising a large proportion of the population, gives testament to this fact. George Barna reports that the number of unchurched adults in the U.S. today has nearly doubled since 1991. The median age of the unchurched adult (38) is lower than the national average (43). Thirty-seven percent of the unchurched are single and have never been married and fifty-five percent are men. Even more astounding is the statistic that nearly thirteen million

GEORGE BARNA REPORTS THAT THE NUMBER OF UNCHURCHED ADULTS IN THE U.S. TODAY HAS NEARLY DOUBLED SINCE 1991.

THE GENERATION GROWING UP IN THE AFTERSHOCKS OF THIS PHENOMENAL CHANGE HAS NO NOTION OF THE WAY THINGS USED TO BE.

people claim to have accepted Jesus Christ as their Savior but do not attend church.[1]

Those of us involved in church leadership—pastors, staff members, small group facilitators, house-church leaders—are seeing the effects of the cultural quakes and eruptions that have taken place. Our old maps—Sunday school, vacation Bible school, church growth formulas, evangelism and outreach campaigns—no longer work as they once did. The generation growing up in the aftershocks of this phenomenal change has no notion of the way things used to be. The number of church attendees among those in their twenties and thirties continues to diminish; they are not coming back to the church as they have in the past. Most do not have a church to return to, as they have never spent significant time in church to begin with.

So where do we find the unchurched of this generation? Drive around some Sunday morning and you will find them, gathered in groups of two to ten, sitting around a table at a bookstore or coffeehouse. They are talking—and listening—to one another. They are experiencing community and seeking intimacy. These locations are not on our Sunday morning maps. If we continue to follow the maps we have always used, we will never reach this generation. They have moved on to land that really wasn't around twenty years ago. Yet we keep searching for the next new program or formula that will bring these spiritually hungry people back to our churches. What a pity. What we need is a compass.

This book isn't about updating our maps—it's about returning to the compass. In his classic novel *Les Misérables*, Victor Hugo tells of the importance of setting our course by compass: "The ocean seeks to lead it astray

SO WHERE DO WE FIND THE UNCHURCHED OF THIS GENERATION?

As pastors, we understand the turmoil church leaders are dealing with today. For the past decade it has become apparent that the modern church models and methods are no longer effective. High control/low accountability church leadership systems are not working. The preoccupation with programs, property, and products is missing the mark. We know you want to see real life-change in your people and to see your church grow. We know you want your church to make a difference in your community and in the world. Jesus showed us the way in his teaching to his disciples 2,000 years ago. It is the only way.

—*Mike & Walt*

in the alarming sameness of its billows, but the vessel has its soul, its compass, which counsels it and always shows it the north." Our compass is Jesus. Just as north is always north, Jesus never changes. As today's church passes through an ocean of cultural changes, it's our Compass that will keep us on course.

Our maps aren't working anymore. We've gotten away from the Compass. That fact can be discussed another day; we don't have time to debate it now. We are not going to share step-by-step what we did to turn our churches around. And we are not going to list everything that is wrong with our culture or write longingly about how we might return to the "good old days." None of that matters. Modernity is over—whether we want it to be or not. The post-modern era is neither good nor evil; it simply is. We do not want to get hung up discussing cultural philosophy and miss what is truly important. All that matters is the compass—Jesus. The Compass is true and will not lie.

WE KEEP SEARCHING FOR THE NEXT NEW PROGRAM OR FORMULA THAT WILL BRING THESE SPIRITUALLY HUNGRY PEOPLE BACK TO OUR CHURCHES. WHAT A PITY. WHAT WE NEED IS A COMPASS.

CHAPTER 1

WHAT'S OUR JOB?

*A*s a leader, you want your church to succeed, to grow. You've no doubt read all the books, attended all the seminars, and listened to all the tapes. Many popular church growth principles fail to effect permanent life change in those who make up the church. They're good principles, but they fall short—like digging a well but stopping before you hit water. We are not asking you to try out a new program. We are not offering new ideas to breathe life into your Sunday mornings. Sitting in church for two hours on Sunday doesn't make people disciples anyway. Instead, we are going to focus on how Jesus lived and told us to live.

We want you to walk confidently as a follower of Jesus across this new cultural terrain and to show those around you how to walk as his followers as well. We are going to show you principles of discipleship that are both memorable and multipliable. Since this was Jesus' approach to ministry, shouldn't it be ours as well?

THERE IS NO "PLAN B"

Jesus left only one plan for church growth: multiplication through disciples making disciples. The amazing thing is Jesus did not have a "Plan B." His last words spoken to his followers were, "You will be my witnesses in

Jerusalem, and in all Judea and Samaria, and to the ends of the earth" (Acts 1:8). He did not offer this as an optional assignment. The future of this new movement rested fully with these disciples. If these few disciples failed to carry out Jesus' instructions, there was no back up plan. Yet we continue to pursue every other method and church growth program to increase our ministries.

Fuller Theological Seminary, the internationally known institution where many have gone to learn principles and methods of church growth, is taking a new look at this discipline. Dr. Eddie Gibbs, the McGavren Professor of Church Growth at Fuller, says traditional church growth curriculum was developed in the 1950s and '60s when Western-based mission

> **SITTING IN CHURCH FOR TWO HOURS ON SUNDAY DOESN'T MAKE PEOPLE DISCIPLES.**

When a man active in our church told me that he just didn't feel connected, that he didn't have a "feeling of intimacy with anyone," I saw clearly what was happening. I had built a church—a large church, successful beyond imagination to most people. But I had lost our community. We didn't need to build a new sanctuary. What we needed to be doing was making disciples. After a lifetime in the ministry, you would think I would know what to do. But I realized I needed help. I decided to look at churches that were successfully making disciples. It was Eddie Gibbs from Fuller Theological Seminary, who told me I should take a look at St. Thomas. When I met the people who attended St. Thomas regularly, I was struck by their depth. They were living in community with one another and demonstrated authentic faith. I came away from that trip convinced I had found what I was looking for. I imagined this to be like it was in the early church. This was discipleship at its best.

—*WALT*

agencies were the driving force in world evangelization and church planting. Gaining members was the measurement device to tell if a church was growing. This, says Gibbs, is no longer the case.

"We have to address the issue of whether numerical church growth also represents a transformation in people's lives and an impact on wider society," says Gibbs. "Ministry must be seen more in terms of 'By the people of God in the world' than 'For the people of God and largely confined to the existing members.'"[2]

Yet in order to have ministry conducted in this manner, these people of God must be sufficiently grounded in grace and truth to meet the onslaught of hate, greed, mistrust, and abuse they will no doubt face. Jesus spent the majority of his time with a handful of chosen ones, teaching them how to follow and make followers. "Make disciples" was his direction to his followers. When he returned to heaven, it was up to these men and women—who were still struggling to "get it"—to multiply or cease to exist.

After my heart attack and six-way bypass in January 2002, I began to consider who might be the successor to my ministry. It would have to be just the right person, someone capable of raising and managing a multi-million dollar budget as well as the staff and programs of a megachurch. It would need to be someone who could effectively reach the twenty- and thirty-year-olds I was struggling to reach.

I discussed this idea with other pastors across the country. But it was in Washington DC that I felt the ground shaking all around me. "Why would anyone want your church?" a pastor there responded. "Anyone who is serious about ministry today does not want to be stuck raising money for maintaining buildings and mortgages. They want to be on the cutting edge making a difference." As hard as it was to hear, I knew what he had just said was right.

— WALT

The same is true today. God has chosen people—not plans or programs—to spread his message. Yet somehow most of our attention and energy has shifted from making disciples to buildings and budgets. We ask our members to spend their time serving as ushers, nursery workers, and committee sitters. When told that Jesus' command is to go and make disciples, we are all too tired from raising money to meet the budget and organizing Wednesday night dinners to fulfill his commission. We have made church a business, and that has distracted us from our real call.

PASTOR, SHEPHERD, OR CEO

Perhaps John Piper has best articulated the problem in his book *Brothers, We Are Not Professionals*. Piper, the senior pastor of Bethlehem Baptist Church in Minneapolis, says the twenty-first century is a great time to be in the ministry. He also says "pastors are being killed by the professionalizing of the pastoral ministry. The mentality of the professional is not the mentality of the prophet. It is not the mentality of the slave of Christ. Professionalism has nothing to do with the essence and heart of the Christian ministry."[3]

According to Piper, the professional's agenda is set by the world, with rewards collected here as well. "Brothers," he writes, "we are not professionals! We are outcasts. We are aliens and exiles in the world (1 Pet. 2:11). Our citizenship is in heaven, and we wait with eager expectation for the Lord (Phil. 3:20). You cannot professionalize the love for His appearing without killing it. And it *is* being killed."[4] Professional ministry doesn't make disciples and that is the only job Jesus gave us. The only one.

> PROFESSIONAL MINISTRY DOES NOT GO WITH MAKING DISCIPLES. AND THAT IS THE ONLY JOB JESUS GAVE US. THE ONLY ONE.

TRANSFORMING YOUR CHURCH

There's a new day dawning with unprecedented opportunities to transform our churches from the inside out. The passionate church is not dead—we simply need to fan the flames into zeal for the kingdom. That's what this book is all about. What will it take to be an effective agent of change in our world? Anyone seeking to be used by God in this emerging culture needs to return to three fundamental skills:

- study the culture,
- read the Bible,
- build the church.

Study the Culture

Learning to be careful observers of the world around us is no new idea to the people of God. The great apostle Paul looked at the temples and sculptures of the great city of Athens before he introduced the Athenian people to "An Unknown God." Throughout the church's history, people have studied and listened to the culture in order to communicate the story in an accessible and understandable way. The twentieth century church found a way to do this.

THROUGHOUT THE CHURCH'S HISTORY PEOPLE HAVE WATCHED AND LISTENED TO THE CULTURE IN ORDER TO COMMUNICATE THE STORY IN AN ACCESSIBLE AND UNDERSTANDABLE WAY.

Today's Christians need to look carefully at the emerging twenty-first century culture. (The artifacts of this culture—television, music, popular books and magazines, the Internet, movies—communicate the hopes, fears, values, and longings of the emerging culture.) We need to rediscover how to communicate the Gospel in a real and relevant way that reaches unreached people where they live.

Read the Bible

CHANGE IS CONSTANT. EITHER THE CHURCH CHANGES OR THE CHURCH DIES.

As we read the Bible we discover the values and vision God has for us. The key value that is communicated through the Scriptures is the message of covenant. At its heart, covenant is a relationship with God brought about by his grace. The Bible gives us a vision of God's kingdom. This is God's mission to the world—his kingdom come and his will done on this earth just as it is in heaven. God is calling his church to reestablish humanity and all creation under his loving rule. These two fundamental themes of Scripture—Kingdom and Covenant—are like the DNA of the Bible, the double helix found throughout God's Word.

Build the Church

The covenant community is made up of kingdom people who together form the church that Jesus is building. We need to recapture the fundamental understanding that Christians do not "go to church," they *are* the church. The simple but profound principles Jesus taught provide both basic discipleship and leadership development. They can be used to point a generation that has lost its bearings to the Compass, and facilitate the building of authentic community in a society where it is fracturing and disintegrating.

Change is constant. Either the church changes or the church dies. Because the world is radically changing, the church must adapt to reach the world. Because Jesus Christ never changes, Christ-followers are equipped to handle radical rapid changes. Throughout history, the church has been going through constant transition. Keeping the faith and focusing on the God-given vision through the stormy seas of change is crucial.

Chapter 2

The Shapes of Discipleship

W e are undeniably in a period of intense cultural quaking. We have moved from the modern era into postmodernity, but not without a great deal of fear and anxiety. As pastors and leaders, we are constantly asking ourselves how we can reach the next generation. One answer is very clear: we cannot continue to do what we have always done and expect to get the results we desire. We must consider their current condition before we can begin to make plans to reach them with help.

A Disoriented Generation

First of all, those who make up the next generation of believers are disoriented. They don't just want a map: they want a life coach. We keep offering them new maps—worship experiences with dimmed lights and candles—when they are crying out for a personal guide. This generation, perhaps like none before it, is desperate for discipleship. The essence of being a disciple is spending time with the teacher himself. And that is just what we get as followers of Jesus—an invitation to his home where we can hang out with him, listen to him,

> WE KEEP OFFERING THEM NEW MAPS— WORSHIP EXPERIENCES WITH DIMMED LIGHTS AND CANDLES— WHEN THEY ARE CRYING OUT FOR A PERSONAL GUIDE.

have him listen to us, become friends. When we present this portrait of Christianity—and there is no other picture that is complete or accurate apart from discipleship—these disoriented, desperate people long to be included in the picture. These young people stay away from our churches not because the message they hear is boring, but because it is shallow. They may be disoriented, but they know that the answer they are looking for is big enough to give them shelter in the time of the next earthquake.

A FEARFUL GENERATION

WHAT CULTURAL "BUILDINGS" DOES THIS GENERATION FEAR? FAMILIES, POLITICAL INSTITUTIONS, AND THE CHURCH.

Anyone who has survived a catastrophic earthquake thinks twice before entering a building again. It seems safer to risk the elements and live outdoors. What cultural "buildings" does this generation fear? Families, political institutions, and the church.

Many members of this generation grew up in broken homes. They know firsthand the devastation of divorce. For them, the family is not a safe institution. There is too much pain associated with it. Christians are not exempt from this. Even those who remain a nuclear family, with mom and dad still married, suffer from the upheaval of the family institution. The atmosphere of hurt and distrust pervades our cultural landscape. The family, Christian or non-Christian, is no longer seen as a landmark that will withstand the shocks of a quake.

Consider how this message is reflected in the media. Until the 1990s, family shows dominated television programming. *Family Ties* and *The Cosby Show,* while not the same as *Leave It to Beaver* or *Father Knows Best,* still had mom and dad working together to provide a safe harbor for their children.

From the '90s to today, those shows have been replaced with others that reflect real life. *Friends* was the number one show of that decade. *Seinfeld* depicted a group of very different people held together not by blood but by loyalty. Thus, community for this generation is no longer defined by family—including ethnic backgrounds or race—but by who will stand with you no matter what. Because the building called "family" crumbled in the quake from the modern world to the postmodern, many are afraid to reenter it.

A Generation Without Identity

This generation is disoriented, afraid of cultural institutions, and without an identity. All that defined who they are was lost in the tremors of postmodernism. Just as those in Napier lost their homes, their jobs, pictures, and mementos that gave them identity, so have the young people of today lost their identity. They are searching diligently for a story to define their lives. The two most influential media today are movies and music. Young people find identities in the stories told on screen and in lyrics. Even if that story does not truly reflect their own, they can adopt it as their own. They see themselves in that story and begin to live it out in real life.

> WE HAVE A STORY THAT CAN SHOW THIS GENERATION WHO THEY ARE ACCORDING TO THEIR CREATOR AND GIVE THEM A CONTEXT FOR LIVING OUT THEIR LIVES.

MTV gets it; so do Nike, Virgin Mobile, and dozens of other companies and their marketing firms. They are spending millions to tell this generation who they are and who they can be—if they only buy their product. They do it for the profit when Christians could be doing it for eternity. We have a story—the greatest story ever told—

that can show this generation who they are according to their Creator and give them a context for living out their lives.

STOP BUILDING MONUMENTS

So, what are we supposed to do in this environment? Do we continue pointing out cultural issues that may or may not have caused the situation we are in? Do we protest and boycott and continue to erect walls between the church and the rest of the world? What about the structure of our churches? How can we continue to think that by holding on to the way it has always been done we will reach the world outside? We are like Peter who, on the mountaintop with Jesus when Moses and Elijah appeared, said, "Let's build monuments so we can hold on to this moment forever." Do you remember God's response? A cloud overshadowed the pinnacle of the mountain, God spoke from the cloud and said, "This is my Son . . . listen to him."

There is no new answer today. There is no need to look beyond what God spoke two thousand years ago. Our only hope is to listen to the Son. Search out what Jesus told his disciples, look for how Jesus walked and talked and conducted himself. We must see that our greatest task as followers of Christ is to go and make more followers.

LIFESHAPES IS DESIGNED TO EQUIP THE BELIEVER FOR KINGDOM LIFE BY LINKING THE DISCIPLESHIP PRINCIPLES OF JESUS TO MEMORABLE IMAGES.

HOW LIFESHAPES CAN HELP

How can simple shapes be used to make disciples who can make disciples? LifeShapes is designed to equip the believer for kingdom life by linking the discipleship principles of Jesus to memorable images—eight shapes. It forms the vocabulary that expresses the theology and daily life of a disciple of Jesus, painting a clear picture through which individuals can gain a greater understanding of what God intends to do in their personal lives, in the church, and in the world.

Most learning in Jesus' day was based on oral tradition. Literacy rates across the Roman Empire were very low and access to written material usually restricted to the elite. People learned through storytelling and verbal teaching rather than reading texts. Their minds were trained to store information and knowledge with accuracy. When Jesus told the disciples to "teach everything I have commanded you," it was expected that they could repeat Jesus' teachings because they learned and remembered them effectively.

The way we learn today is much different. Trying to convey aspects of discipleship through lists, principles, and phrases does not work in our time. This generation is visually oriented. For instance, when you look at the three intersecting circles above, what immediately comes to mind?

LIFESHAPES IS NOT A WAY TO TEACH AND APPLY THOUSANDS OF BIBLICAL PRINCIPLES. RATHER, IT IS A FEW KEY CONCEPTS THAT WILL MAKE LIFELONG LEARNERS OF THOSE YOU DISCIPLE.

If you thought "Mickey Mouse," congratulations! That is what most people think of when they see these three overlapping circles. Now think of all the bits of information and emotional responses that single image conjures up for you. Perhaps you can recite some of the lines from a Disney movie or describe its plot in detail. Or you can share about a family trip to one of Disney's theme parks, your favorite ride there, how you felt after that day.

LifeShapes employs this same principle. It's a simple way to learn and remember a lot of information. Even more amazing is how easily and quickly LifeShapes students become teachers. We saw this illustrated when a team of young adults from St. Thomas went on a mission to São Paulo, Brazil. Tim, a member of the team, had just completed the LifeShapes course a few weeks before. Once we arrived in São Paulo, he began sharing the Circle with a Brazilian worker over coffee, the Semi-Circle and Triangle over lunch, and the Square and Pentagon over dinner. Tim the disciple was discipling others.

LifeShapes is not a way to teach and apply thousands of biblical principles. Rather, it is a few key concepts that will make lifelong learners of those you disciple. Disciples are those who have a new framework of truth, enabling them to build biblical principles into their lives and grow together in authentic community. This is the whole aim of LifeShapes. When LifeShapes works under the empowering of the Holy Spirit, we can make disciples who in turn make other disciples, thus building community in the process. As we introduce you to LifeShapes in the chapters that follow, we pray that this will be your experience and that you will share your experience with others.

THE CIRCLE

THE CIRCLE HELPS US IDENTIFY
THE SIGNIFICANT EVENTS OF OUR LIVES
IN A WAY THAT ENABLES US TO MOVE DEEPER
IN THE DIRECTION OF GOD'S WILL.

CHAPTER 3

IT'S ABOUT TIME

After John was put in prison, Jesus went into Galilee, proclaiming the good news of God. 15*"The time has come," he said. "The kingdom of God is near. Repent and believe the good news!"*

—Mark 1:14–15

J esus called people to follow him, calling those people disciples. *Disciple* means "learner." But what does this look like in practice? The call to be a disciple involves a daily process of laying down your life to follow Jesus. But how do we know when God is at work in our lives? Does the Bible give any insights as to how to process the situations and issues that arise in daily life? How does God guide us?

KAIROS INTERRUPTED

The use of the word *time* in the New Testament is an interesting study. No doubt you remember from your Greek classes that several words in the Greek language translate into the English word for time. *Chronos* is the one we would find most familiar, meaning successive or sequential time, the

One of the most astonishing things I noticed about St. Thomas, Mike's church in Sheffield, England, was that the people there seemed to use a whole other language when talking to one another. In, Out, and Up. The D2s. Several people were chatting together about the "*kairos* moments" of their week. I soon realized that they were using *kairos*, the Greek word for time in Mark 1:15, to describe events they had encountered in their week—events that made them pause and reconsider their spiritual life. This way of applying biblical principles in new ways is one of the things I find so attractive about the LifeShapes pattern for discipleship.

— *WALT*

kind of time you find on your wristwatch. Another is *kairos*, meaning an event, an opportunity—a moment in time when perhaps everything changes because it is the right time. Perhaps a *kairos* moment is when the circumstances of your life are brought together in the bottleneck of time. *Kairos* is the eternal God breaking into your circumstances with an event that will gather the loose ends of your life and knot them together in his hands. In *kairos* moments, the rules of *chronos* time seem to be suspended.

KAIROS IS THE ETERNAL GOD BREAKING INTO YOUR CIRCUMSTANCES WITH AN EVENT THAT WILL GATHER THE LOOSE ENDS OF YOUR LIFE AND KNOT THEM TOGETHER IN HIS HANDS.

Kairos Events Can Be Positive or Negative

Do you remember the day you were married? How about the birth of your first child? Think about a favorite vacation you took with your family. These are all *kairos* moments where you cherished every minute. Some *kairos* events, however, leave an impact because of their tragic consequences. The death of a loved one, a divorce, an argument with a co-worker, the horrific events of September 11, 2001: *kairos* events are rarely neutral.

Kairos Moments Can Be Recognized by the Impact They Leave on You

Perhaps you announce a building project at your church. Instead of the expected enthusiastic response, you are greeted with silence and stares. After the service, the people shuffle out quickly. You notice the whispers and the fingers pointed back at you. You feel anxiety and fear. You are passing through a *kairos* moment. Your emotions are often a great indicator of *kairos* events, and it is often the negative events producing negative emotions that present the greatest potential for growth.

Kairos Events Signal Opportunities to Grow

This growth occurs on an individual level and on a corporate level. Perhaps your church is experiencing a *kairos* event even now: changes in your staff, loss of a facility, unexpected growth. Or perhaps there was a *kairos* event in your church past—one that might serve as an entry point into

I was leading a successful church in England when God introduced a *kairos* moment that would impact our entire congregation. We had been using a nightclub as our meeting place, drawing a thousand people on a Sunday. I realized God was saying, "What would you do if you lost the building? Get everyone ready." Then one day, health and safety shut down the facility. Within two weeks, we were out—and I was away in New Zealand at the time. But because we as a church chose to see this *kairos* event as an opportunity for growth, we planted seventeen congregations in one weekend and the church grew—financially and numerically. Everyone involved faced his or her own *kairos* moments, going through the Learning Circle many times, but the resulting spiritual and personal growth was phenomenal.

—*MIKE*

the learning process. As you and your church learn to recognize *kairos* moments as God's interventions, you will be able to enter the Learning Circle, and experience growth. You will be able to seize these opportunities and celebrate the kingdom life this process brings.

THE CIRCLE OF LIFE

THERE IS A PORTAL IN TIME THAT WE CAN'T SEE, AND THE IN-BREAKING OF GOD'S PRESENCE IS ABOUT TO TAKE PLACE.

What does the Bible say about a lifestyle of learning? When you're looking for it, quite a lot, actually. As a matter of fact, Jesus' first teaching was on this subject.

"The time has come. The kingdom of God is near. Repent and believe the good news" (Mark 1:14–15).

This verse, which could be called a summary statement of the teaching of Jesus, says a lot more about learning than first meets the eye. In essence, Jesus is saying a great opportunity is available: God's kingdom is within reach for all of us. *The kingdom of God is near* literally means that if you reach in the right direction, your hand will disappear through the curtain of this world and reappear in the reality of the next world. There is a portal in time that we can't see, and the in-breaking of God's presence is about to take place. The Learning Circle suggests a framework by which we can process what God is saying to us in the *kairos* event and learn how to respond in a way that enables us to grow in our discipleship.

The Circle shows us:

- what it means to live a lifestyle of learning as a disciple of Christ;
- how to recognize important events as opportunities for growth; and
- how to process these events.

CHOOSING TO LEARN FROM LIFE

We leaders tend to be an analytical lot. We tend to think of our journey of faith as linear; it has a starting point (salvation) and an ending point (heaven).

Salvation ●————————————————● Heaven

Scripture would seem to indicate that a disciple's relationship with God is more dynamic. Let us suggest another picture. Here is a believer, walking what he considers to be a straight, linear path. Perhaps he has a purpose in mind; perhaps he is just walking in the direction he thinks is best. Then, seemingly out of the blue, a *kairos* moment (X) takes place.

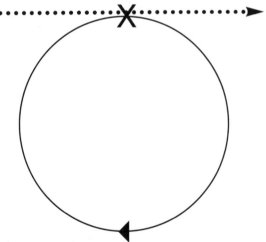

He can react in many different ways. He can keep walking, ignoring the open door for growth. He can stop. He can go backward. Or he can enter the Learning Circle. Jesus extends a great opportunity to anyone who would seek to know him and follow him. God's kingdom is within reach—but to access it we need to go through the process of repentance and belief.

CHAPTER 4

A LIFESTYLE OF LEARNING

When a *kairos* moment occurs, we often want to study all the events that led up to it with the hope of preventing a similar thing from happening again. But we are looking through the wrong end of the telescope. Instead of looking back, we need to look forward to the growth we can experience because of what has happened. *Kairos* moments are God-given opportunities to enter into a process of learning kingdom living.

KEYS TO THE KINGDOM

"The time has come," [Jesus] said. "The kingdom of God is near. Repent and believe the good news!" (Mark 1:15).

The Circle represents our journey into the kingdom of God. To enter the kingdom, however, we must go through a process of repentance and belief. The process can be difficult and challenging and, more often than not, painful. It is through this process we learn how to lay down our lives and pick up the cross.

What propels us into this learning process is a *kairos* event. As we discussed in chapter 3, it can be positive (a promotion at work) or negative (getting laid off from your job). It can be big (your wedding)

> Working with Walt, I've been impressed by his teachable spirit. Here he is pastor of a very large church; he's written a number of books; he receives requests to preach at any number of churches and conferences. Yet he has a humble spirit. It's not enough to recognize *kairos* moments, you have to be willing, as Walt is, to learn from them as well.
>
> —*MIKE*

or small (a date night with your spouse). Generally speaking, *kairos* moments are not neutral, as they leave an impression on us. But when a *kairos* moment occurs, we must decide to enter the Circle. From the moment we do so, we are in a learning mode.

Two key words in the Mark passage help define the learning process: *repent* and *believe*. You will remember that the word *repent* is from the Greek *metanoia*, meaning to change one's mind. As church leaders, we often encounter strong resistance when we say *repent* because of its unfortunate association with negative messages of condemnation without the grace. Our people will respond differently when they realize that *metanoia* simply means a change of heart that shows up in a lifestyle or behavior change. Walking as a disciple of Jesus means constantly growing and changing inwardly as you take on more of the character of the Teacher. Change is not an option: it is a vital part of the life of a follower of Jesus. Once we change on the inside, the new attitude will affect our outward actions.

Where *kairos* is an event word—something that has a beginning and ending—repentance (*metanoia*) is a process word, as is believe (*pistis*). The Circle is a process, a way of living that does not have a specific beginning and ending. One does not become a disciple of Jesus and stand still; discipleship is a lifestyle of learning. And this learning begins with a change of heart.

Entering the Learning Circle

Having experienced a *kairos* event in our lives, we then begin the process of learning from it. There is a widely known Learning Circle that involves just three steps: observe, reflect, and act. The LifeShapes Circle has uniquely expanded this to six. There are three parts in the repent process (observe, reflect, and discuss) and three parts to the believe process (plan, account, and act).

The first part of the repent process is observation. To change our lives, we need to observe where we are. When a *kairos* moment stops us in our tracks, this is the time to observe our reactions, our emotions, our thoughts. We must be honest in our observations—see things as they are—if we are to change inwardly.

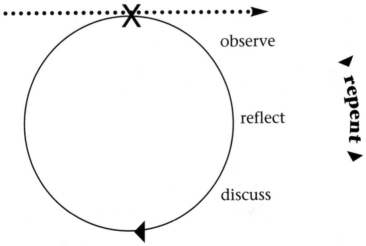

Once we observe our condition, we need to reflect. Reflect on what? Reflect on our observations. We need to ask ourselves why we reacted as we did, why we feel as we do, why a certain event brought these emotions to the surface. Asking questions is a great way to reflect. Again, our answers must be honest if real change is to take place.

WHEN A *KAIROS* MOMENT STOPS US IN OUR TRACKS, THIS IS THE TIME TO OBSERVE OUR REACTIONS, OUR EMOTIONS, OUR THOUGHTS.

(By the way, introverts will find this stage more natural than extroverts as it requires spending time alone in reflection.)

If observing and reflecting are to lead to lasting change, we must invite others into the process with us. For repentance to take hold, we've got to share it with someone else. It is important that we have others in our lives we can discuss our observations and reflections with, and who will be honest in their response to us. These people must be strong enough to handle confession, be it small or large, and share God's grace and forgiveness with us. These are trustworthy friends, who will stand with us, pray with us, fight alongside of us, but will not flatter us with empty words. "Therefore confess your sins to each other and pray for each other so that you may be healed" (James 5:16). ▲

Repentance is necessary if we are to grow as disciples, but it is not always easy. Facing our failings, our pain, and our fears is something we want to put off, like a trip to the dentist or bathing the cat. As we step into the process of observing, reflecting on, and discussing our sins and shortcomings with others, we are not only opening up the ugliness of our lives for others to see, we are opening it up for *us* to see.

FOR REPENTANCE TO TAKE HOLD, YOU'VE GOT TO SHARE IT WITH SOMEONE ELSE. IT IS IMPORTANT THAT WE HAVE OTHERS IN OUR LIVES WE CAN DISCUSS OUR OBSERVATIONS AND REFLECTIONS WITH, AND WHO WILL BE HONEST IN THEIR RESPONSE TO US.

In a culture where our disciples look to our example and where our own pride often gets the best of us, we find ourselves running away from the sins and faults of our lives and toward the goal of fixing the problems in the lives of others. This is the picture that many of

▲ FOR MORE ON IN, SEE THE TRIANGLE, CHAPTER 11.

us paint rather than simply becoming authentic in our relationship with God.

The image of a leader who is constantly trying to flee from his anguish and fear; hoping that if he runs far enough or flies fast enough, he can somehow make it all go away is not the image of repentance that we are called to embrace. Dr. Larry Crabb wrote, "A spiritual community consists of people who have the integrity to come clean. It is compromised of those who own their shortcomings and failures because they hate them more than they hate the shortcomings and failures of others, who therefore discover that a well of pure water flows beneath their most fetid corruption."[5]

What a great picture of discipleship: abandoning ourselves to the forgiveness of God, walking in his grace, and creating a safe place within our church communities for others to do the same. This only comes, however, if *we* are willing to walk first in the footsteps of repentance.

CHAPTER 5

LIFE IS LIKE A SLINKY

What good is it, my brothers, if a man claims to have faith but has no deeds? . . .
17. . . faith by itself, if it is not accompanied by action, is dead. 18But someone will
say, "You have faith; I have deeds." Show me your faith without deeds, and I will
show you my faith by what I do.

—James 2:14; 17–18

*J*ust because we experience something—in other words, just because we go through a *kairos* moment—does not mean we learn anything. And repenting will not by itself bring about change. Repentance is only the first part of the Circle. Stopping after we repent only invites the experience to return and makes it harder to repent the next time.

After recognizing the issue, assessing why it happened, and discussing it with someone else, in the process of rethinking and repenting before God, we must move to the left side of the Circle and begin believing change is possible. Faith is the second half of our Circle, the next process in the lifestyle of discipleship.

Do a Google search on "faith" and one of the first sites listed takes you to where you can buy Faith Shoes online. Founded in 1964 by Samuel Faith, it is, according their web site, "the number one destination for shoe addicts with a passion for fashion."

This is not the faith we are talking about, but it reflects truth.

In my early years as a pastor, I was so intent on building the church that I directed all my prime time and energy there. My family got what was left over. Time and again I would tell my wife, Mary, that I would be home by six for dinner, but too often I allowed the demands, needs, and crises of the church to take priority. I would arrive home late to find my dinner cold and my wife hot.

The church was my mistress. Mary found it hard to compete with God's work. We were trapped in a vicious cycle: Mary would confront me, and I would repent, but I failed to implement the change I promised.

One night, as I again prepared to go out, even though I had promised to stay at home, Mary told me, "If you come back late again to our house, you won't find me in it." This was a *kairos* moment I could not afford to ignore. This time I would go full circle: we planned a date night, asked our church to hold us accountable, and it's been working well ever since.

— WALT

"Faith," says the writer of Hebrews, "is the substance of things believed." It is a substance—something real and tangible, just like Faith Shoes. It is not simply a nice belief, but substantive display of belief. Faith that cannot be seen, writes James, is no faith at all. Faith is action, and right action will take us into the kingdom.

There are some who say that faith is spelled R-I-S-K. We disagree. If you are acting in faith, you are simply doing what you know God wills to be done. There is no risk in doing God's will. (There is, however, great risk in ignoring God and doing what we want to do.) If you need an alternative spelling for faith, you can use these four letters: S-U-R-E.

Just as there are three spokes in the wheel of repentance (observe, reflect, discuss), there are three spokes for faith. The first is to plan. On the basis of our observation, reflection, and discussion, we need to make a plan to lead our inner change.

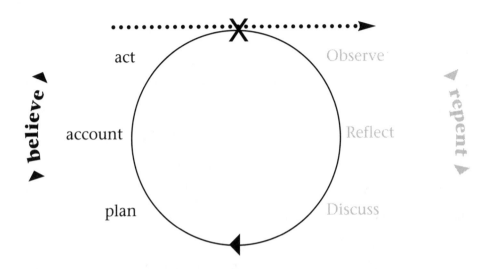

For example, if your growing credit card debt has finally escalated to the point of crisis and, in reflecting on the cause, the Lord reveals an emptiness or void you are trying to fill through shopping, have a strategy for recognizing the feelings that lead to binge shopping and for reacting in the proper way. Or if God has shown you that you need to respond with more encouragement to a staff member, develop concrete plans of when and how.

Planning nearly always involves seeking the kingdom of God first, no matter what the issue. Most of us find that ultimately our *kairos* events lead us to discover we have used someone or something as a substitute for God. If shopping is your substitute, make a plan to buy only necessities, to pay only cash, and then to let the Lord fill the emptiness within.

BEING AFRAID TO SHARE WITH SOME- ONE ELSE BECAUSE YOU THINK YOUR THOUGHTS OR FEELINGS ARE TOO PRIVATE WILL KEEP YOU FROM GROWING AND CHANGING.

If a plan is to succeed, it is important to have at least one person hold us accountable to it. We need to externalize the things that have been going on internally.

Change doesn't happen in private. Being afraid to share with someone else because you think your thoughts or feelings are too private will keep you from growing and changing. All the mistakes the heroes in the Bible made are eternally public. Just think how Peter feels today seeing people read and discuss how he denied Jesus. Accountability is important to Jesus, shown by his sending out the disciples in groups of two. Sharing your inner thoughts and outward failings with another person may be hard at first, but it is ultimately necessary if we are to grow. The Circle will not turn correctly if one spoke is left out or broken off. We cannot skip accountability and still say we are disciples of Christ. It is that simple.

Once a plan is made and a relationship of accountability established, the

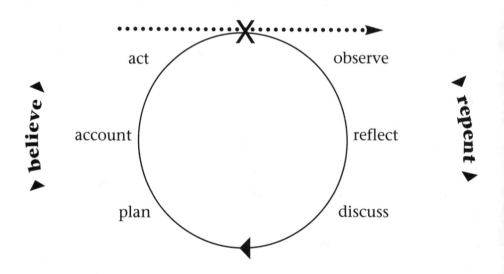

natural reaction is for action to take place. Faith always comes to the surface and always produces action. It cannot be contained. Thoughts and intents that are held within and not acted upon are not faith, no matter what we like to say. ("My faith is personal" is a favorite. But that is a self-contradicting statement. Faith is always acted out, never kept bottled up within.)

> FAITH ALWAYS COMES TO THE SURFACE AND ALWAYS PRODUCES ACTION. IT CANNOT BE CONTAINED.

THE CIRCLE ON THE MOUNT

Here is a biblical example of the Circle. Jesus and his followers are just wrapping up a long day. He goes up on a hillside and teaches what we now call the Sermon on the Mount. In this daylong teaching, Jesus outlines the radical lifestyle that he calls his followers to adopt. He talks about such things as murder, adultery, divorce, lying, revenge, loving your enemy, giving to the needy, prayer and fasting, and the love of money. As the people listen, they probably begin experiencing the kind of internal pressure that leads to a *kairos* event. (When this occurs, it can lead to anxiety and worry.) So Jesus addresses the situation.

"Do not worry about your life, what you will eat or drink; or about your body, what you will wear. Is not life more important than food, or the body more important than clothes?" (Matt. 6:25). An event has taken place. It causes worry, anxiety, stress. The disciples need to learn about the problem of worrying from this event so Jesus begins with observation.

"Look at the birds of the air; they do not sow or reap or store away in barns, and yet your heavenly Father feeds them" (Matt. 6:26). Having revealed what is happening in his followers' hearts, Jesus takes them through the process that will set them free. First he tells them to look at the birds. No doubt this makes them wonder. Jesus is leading his disciples to observe their own lives by having them look at something else they can understand. The birds of the air do not sow or reap or store away in barns, and yet their heavenly Father feeds them. This is a simple, straightforward observation, and it helps the disciples recognize their own fears and lack of faith. Likewise, observing our *kairos* event leads to examining ourselves.

Reflection begins when Jesus asks, "Are you not much more valuable than they?" (Matt. 6:26). This, of course, is a rhetorical question to which the answer is yes. (Asking questions is the best way to facilitate reflection.) Birds are valuable, but we are more valuable. Jesus is helping the disciples put things into perspective.

Reflection leads to conversation and discussion. "Who of you by worrying can add a single hour to his life? And why do you worry about clothes?" (Matt. 6:27–28). There is no record of a discussion between Jesus and his disciples at this point, but the usual method for teaching in that day was question and answer. Discussion was a basic part of the learning experience; therefore it is safe to assume this teaching included discussion that Matthew chose not to record. People need to talk things over with others in order to find clarity. We try to change the things we worry about, but Jesus says the person who worries is the one who needs to change. Change happens to us when we try to answer searching questions such as "Why am I worrying about this when I know God is in control?"

MAKING PLANS ON THE BASIS OF THE KINGDOM, IN RIGHT RELATIONSHIP WITH GOD, MEANS THE WORRIES OF TOMORROW NEED NOT DOMINATE US.

"But seek first his kingdom and his righteousness, and all these things will be given to you as well" (Matt. 6:33). How do we build a life that is not based on worry but founded on faith? This verse illustrates the importance of planning. Planning is built around a vision. We plan to attain something. Jesus tells us to make plans to seek his kingdom and his righteousness. *Righteousness* means *right relationship*. Making plans on the basis of the kingdom, in right relationship with God, means the worries of tomorrow need not dominate us. God will take care of everything—including us! This is the essence of our vision: to make Jesus the true Lord of our lives.

To conclude this message, Jesus tells us we should be accountable for the way we live, speak, and think. "Do not judge, or you too will be judged" (Matt. 7:1). Don't live your life continuously calling other people to account for their actions. Instead, live your life in the recognition that you will be called to account. Hypocrites look for faults in others and miss their own faults. Jesus calls us to be accountable to one another.

> DON'T LIVE YOUR LIFE CONTINUOUSLY CALLING OTHER PEOPLE TO ACCOUNT FOR THEIR ACTIONS. INSTEAD, LIVE YOUR LIFE IN THE RECOGNITION THAT YOU WILL BE CALLED TO ACCOUNT.

He then tells a story of two men building houses—one on sand, the other on rock. We often place the emphasis of this story on our building our own houses, or lives, on Jesus our Rock. But what Jesus emphasizes is hearing his words and acting on them. The wise man listens to what Jesus says—and then acts upon it.

LIVING LIKE A SLINKY

Once you are aware of the Circle—and put it into practice—your life can look like a Slinky, a series of loops held together by time. Each time round the Circle means you have grown a little more and taken on a little more of the character of Christ. Our lives are really about events connected together over time and our response to these events. The correct response—repent

SKIPPING ONE OR MORE OF THE STEPS IN THE CIRCLE MEANS YOU WILL MORE THAN LIKELY CONTINUE TO STRUGGLE OVER AND OVER AGAIN WITH THE SAME ISSUE.

and believe—leads us more fully into the kingdom. Skipping one or more of the steps in the Circle means you will more than likely continue to struggle over and over again with the same issue.

How do we take up the cross and become wholly devoted students following Jesus? Surrender to the process of change. Embrace the fruit of the Spirit he wants to grow in our lives. And when it gets hard to face the issues of sin that will ultimately surface in your life, push through. Don't turn back and look for relief from the internal struggle. The rewards will be great if you persevere. In fact, once you have tasted of the goodness of the Lord, like the man who found the pearl of great price, you will sell everything you have to keep it and know it more fully.

Following are examples of Jesus and the disciples employing the Circle.

The Epileptic (Matthew 17:14–21; Mark 9:14–29)
The epileptic seizure (*kairos*)
Unbelieving and perverse generation! (observe and reflect)
Lord, why couldn't we drive it out? (discuss)
This kind can only come out by prayer (plan)
Mustard seed principle (account/act)

Forgiving Wrongs (Matthew 18:15–20; Matthew 18:21–35)
A wrong is done, a resentment remembered (*kairos*)
If your brother sins, go to him (observe and reflect)
Lord, how many times? (discuss)
Therefore, forgive your brother from the heart (plan, account, act)

A Mother's Request for Status (Matthew 20:20–28)

Coming to Jesus with request (*kairos*)

When other disciples hear this they are indignant (observe and reflect)

Jesus calls them together for teaching and discussion (discuss)

Not so with you! (plan)

Whoever wants to be first must be a slave to all (account and act)

The Rich Young Man (Matthew 19:16–29)

Conversation (*kairos*)

When the disciples hear, they are astonished (observe and reflect)

Who can be saved? (reflect)

We left everything; what will there be for us? (discuss)

If you leave houses, family, fields (plan, account, act)

THE SEMI-CIRCLE

WE CAN REDISCOVER THE RHYTHM OF LIFE
THE CREATOR GOD INTENDED FOR US
IN THE PRINCIPLES OF THE SEMI-CIRCLE.

CHAPTER 6

LIVING IN RHYTHM WITH LIFE

*T*he very first commandment given to us by God was to "be fruitful and multiply." We were not created just simply to exist. Our Creator expects us to produce an increase. Jesus told a story about three servants, each given an amount of money from their master. Two of the servants worked with the money to create a good return on their investments, while the third—called wicked and lazy when his master heard his story—sat on the money and did not produce an increase. The two who returned more than they started with were rewarded, while the one who gave back only what he was given was punished. Clearly we are not to be lazy and wicked servants; we were made to bear fruit.

But does this mean we are to be workaholics? Apparently many church leaders think so. Statistics bear the results of the work-round-the-clock attitude many

I have found the principles of the Semi-Circle to have a profound effect on people, especially those in ministry. I remind them about how God created Adam and Eve and told them to be fruitful. They all nod in agreement. Good honest work is a blessing. But look at what they did on their first full day. God created Adam on the sixth day. What happened on the seventh day? They rested. Thus we see this principle in place: we work from our rest, not rest from our work. This can be life-changing stuff!

—MIKE

STUDIES SUGGEST THAT MORE THAN A THOUSAND PASTORS QUIT THEIR CHURCHES EVERY MONTH. IF THIS IS NOT EVIDENCE OF AN EPIDEMIC OF VOCATIONAL BURNOUT, WE DON'T KNOW WHAT IS.

pastors have adopted. Studies suggest that more than a thousand pastors quit their churches every month. If this is not evidence of an epidemic of vocational burnout, we don't know what is.

PRODUCTIVITY, STRESS, AND MEMORY FOAM

We all have stress in our lives, but it is not always bad stress. Stress, as we recall from our high school physics class, is simply force applied to an object to change its shape or course. Stress fractures occur when the object is unmoving or unbending. The right amount of stress on a violin string creates a beautiful note. Too little stress results in a maddening buzz; too much stress produces a shrill off-key sound. We can't—and shouldn't—try to avoid stress. It is part of life. But we are not made to bear too much stress.

Studies estimate that forty-three percent of adults suffer adverse health effects from stress, and stress-related ailments account for seventy-five to ninety percent of all doctor's visits.[6] It is estimated that the number of stress-related deaths in the UK at 180,000 each year. Why do we stand for this level of stress in our lives?

This pressure-filled lifestyle is just as prevalent among Christians. We may proclaim, "Cast your cares on him, for he cares for you," but we don't live it ourselves. We quote from Matthew, "My yoke is easy and my burden is light," but we continue to pack heavy burdens on our backs. Something has gone very wrong.

God designed us to be productive. But we build our identities around our activities. We are not living in the truth of who God created us to be.

We have become human "doings" rather than human "beings." We need a biblical framework for a rhythm of life that allows us to be fruitful in balance with being at rest. We need to be secure in who we are, based on what Christ did for us on the cross and the very great promises we have that we are loved and accepted by him. We must stop striving to gain the acceptance of others by what we do, leading to a driven lifestyle.

> WE HAVE BECOME HUMAN "DOINGS" RATHER THAN HUMAN "BEINGS."

We see in Scripture a pattern of life we are destined to live from the time of our birth. We can see it in the lives of Adam and Eve before the fall, and we see it lived out on a daily basis by Jesus. This is the pattern of life we call the Semi-Circle, so called from a picture of a pendulum swinging in a natural rhythm.

Rest   Work

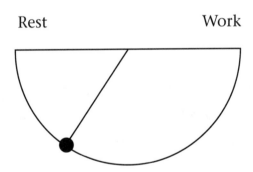

26Then God said, "Let us make man in our image, in our likeness, and let them rule over the fish of the sea and the birds of the air, over the livestock, over all the earth, and over all the creatures that move along the ground." 27So God created man in his own image, in the image of God he created him; male and female he created them. 28 God blessed them and said to them, "Be fruitful and increase in

number; fill the earth and subdue it. Rule over the fish of the sea and the birds of the air and over every living creature that moves on the ground." ²⁹Then God said, "I give you every seed-bearing plant on the face of the whole earth and every tree that has fruit with seed in it. They will be yours for food. ³⁰And to all the beasts of the earth and all the birds of the air and all the creatures that move on the ground—everything that has the breath of life in it—I give every green plant for food." And it was so. ³¹God saw all that he had made, and it was very good. And there was evening, and there was morning—the sixth day. ¹Thus the heavens and the earth were completed in all their vast array. ²By the seventh day God had finished the work he had been doing; so on the seventh day he rested from all his work. ³ And God blessed the seventh day and made it holy, because on it he rested from all the work of creating that he had done.

—Genesis 1:26–2:3

¹⁵*The* LORD *God took the man and put him in the Garden of Eden to work it and take care of it.*

—Genesis 2:15

⁸*Then the man and his wife heard the sound of the* LORD *God as he was walking in the garden in the cool of the day, and they hid from the* LORD *God among the trees of the garden. ⁹But the* LORD *God called to the man, "Where are you?"*

—Genesis 3:8–9

We see in Genesis that on the sixth day, God created man in his image. We need to stop here and consider the word *image*—it is very important in our understanding of the Semi-Circle. To us, *image* brings the idea of a reflection in a mirror or a portrait reflecting the likeness of someone. If a picture taken by a photographer shows a person's face, we say it is a good image of that person. But these thoughts would not have been in the mind of those who first heard these words. When Moses first composed these words, there were no mirrors, no portrait painters, and no one-hour photo labs. In those days, a person would get a reference point for how he or she looked by looking at others. But this is not the meaning of the image spoken of in Genesis 1. A better word would be *imprint* or *impression.* It is the picture of God leaving his handprint on us when he fashioned us from clay. There is an indentation on us that can only be filled by the hand of God. Yet from the fall of man onward, we have been pulling away from the touch of our Creator, trying to fill the imprints with all sorts of insufficient fixes. This was seen from the very beginning with the first man and woman—our ancestors.

Have you seen memory foam mattresses? You can place your hand on the top of the mattress, and the imprint made stays there for some time. This is an impression that can only be totally filled with the hand that made it. This is the same with us. We have an impression in our lives that can only be filled by the hand that made it. (But the impression God puts on us never fades away.)

Working to Be Human

God is walking in the garden he created in the cool of the evening. He desired the company of those he made, Adam and Eve. The indication from the text is that this was a regular event, a routine in their daily lives. At the end of the day the Lord would turn up and expect his beloved ones to be there to go on a stroll with him. God made himself visible each evening so Adam and Eve could feel connected to their Father. It was a daily reminder that God's hand filled the imprint on each of them. This was how it was meant to be between the Creator and the created since the beginning of our time. This time of retreat and rest following a day of labor was not an optional "if you have time but if not don't worry about it" event. It was built into us. It is how God created us to live.

But on this evening our fore parents failed to show up. They were hiding from the Hand that alone could fill them and make them feel complete. After a confrontation with God, they were cursed to work among thorns and thistles, sweating in the heat from backbreaking labor. But this is not how it was supposed to be.

Work itself is not a curse. Before the fall, before Adam and Eve decided to go it alone without the hand of God in their lives (this phrase takes on a whole new meaning when you picture the imprint of God on us, doesn't it?), God had given them instructions on how to care for the garden. Work was assigned before the fall. We were designed for intentional activity to produce a sense of fruitfulness in our lives. This leads us to several conclusions.

1. *Unemployment causes our lives to fall below what is standard.* When people become unemployed, it's as though they have fallen from their God-given call to lead productive lives. That's why people struggle so much when they lose their jobs. The focus of productivity and fruitfulness in their lives is lost; it's as though they stop being fully human. No wonder depression often accompanies unemployment.

2. *There is no such thing as retirement.* If you leave your job voluntarily, it will not be long before you begin feeling the onset of depression. No amount of golf or fishing can take the place of being fruitful. And don't even get us started on sitting all day in front of the

television. If you stop all productive activity in your life, you are pulling away from your God-designed calling. You cannot live a successful life as a human. In fact, many people die within a year or two of retirement because they cease to be fruitful.

In the movie *Secondhand Lions*, Hub and Garth (played brilliantly by Michael Caine and Robert Duvall)—brothers and former fighters in the French Foreign Legion—have retired to Texas. When fiery, hot-tempered Hub overexerts himself he suffers a blackout spell that lands him briefly in the hospital. After checking Hub out, the brothers stop at a diner and order barbecue. Garth begins probing to see what is bothering Hub.

Garth: "What's the matter, brother? Are you afraid of dying?"

Hub: "Hell, no, I'm not afraid of dying."

Garth: "Then what is it?"

Hub: "I'm afraid of being useless."[7]

It is not until Hub finds a new purpose—raising his great-nephew, Walter—that he recovers his will to live.

3. *There must be work in heaven.* If you were counting on sitting in an endless church service, sorry. There was work before the fall; therefore there must be work after the redemption. This life is a foreshadowing of the real life yet to come.

Work is a strategic part of human existence. We are to live productive lives or we will fall away from our God-given calling and the standard of basic humanity. We were created on the sixth day of creation in order to work. But even more important is what happened on the seventh day.

CHAPTER 7

WORKING FROM REST

Work is important, as we have just seen. We were created to be fruitful and productive. Work is a natural part of life and should be celebrated more often than once a year on Labor Day. That being said, we cannot be productive workers if we do not live in the Semi-Circle balance of work and rest.

God created man and woman on the sixth day, setting them in a garden full of wild, wonderful creatures and delicious foods. He gave them instruction on caring for the animals and plants in the garden. He told them to be fruitful. But on the first full day of existence for Adam and Eve, God rested. All of creation took a well-deserved break in activity. This was our first full day, a day of rest. Then the work began. From this we see an important principle of life: we are to work from our rest, not rest from our work.

MURDER, ADULTERY, WORK

Rest is God's healthy starting point for us. We are human beings, not human doings. This is the order God has established for us: rest, then work. But we have it backward. We pride ourselves on our strong work ethic, even using it as a sign of godliness. The true sign of godliness—imitating God—is to pattern our life after him. And for God, rest is vitally important. As a

As a youth worker in Hackney, I was all fired up. I was going to go out and prove myself. My pastor predicted that I would run out of steam. In fact, he put aside money in an envelope for when I did crash and burn. And I did! About nine months in, I woke up one day, looked into the mirror, and saw an old man staring back at me. When I arrived in tears at the pastor's house, he handed me the envelope and told me to come back when I was ready. For days I rode the buses around Sheffield, reading until God broke through and I realized that I couldn't do it in my own strength. I need times of rest and retreat if I am to be fruitful.

—*MIKE*

matter of fact, rest from our activities is listed in God's Top Ten. The commandment to keep the Sabbath is right up there with "don't kill," "don't steal," and "don't commit adultery." In other words, being a workaholic is, to God, just as bad as being a murderer or adulterer. Rest is not an option if we are to walk in the lifestyle of a disciple.

Since our first experience as created beings with our Creator was a day of rest, we see that in order to fulfill our calling to be fruitful, we must start from a place of rest. Resting in God—abiding in his presence—is the only way we can be successful in what he has called us to do. Yet how many of us schedule days of rest and relaxation on the calendar before we schedule meetings, conventions, and other days of work? Is this challenging to you?

You are facing pressure to be successful in your ministry. You are searching for ways to grow your church, build your small group, reach more people with the Good News. This is good—you are meant to be fruitful. God wants your ministry to grow more than you do. Growth is a sign of life. But in order to be productive, as God wants you to be, you must live in the rhythm of the Semi-Circle.

THE PENDULUM SWING

Imagine a pendulum swinging in rhythm—back and forth, to and fro. The shape created by this swinging pendulum is a Semi-Circle. At one end of the pendulum's arc is fruitfulness. At the other end is abiding. We can't have one without the other. We abide in Christ, then go forth to bear fruit. We bear fruit; then we are pruned back and enter a time of abiding. Rest, work, work, rest. It is a rhythm we see in nature as well.

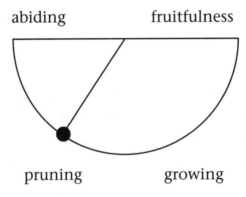

abiding   *fruitfulness*

pruning   *growing*

¹*"I am the true vine, and my Father is the gardener. ²He cuts off every branch in me that bears no fruit, while every branch that does bear fruit he prunes so that it will be even more fruitful. ³You are already clean because of the word I have spoken to you. ⁴Remain in me, and I will remain in you. No branch can bear fruit by itself; it must remain in the vine. Neither can you bear fruit unless you remain in me. ⁵"I am the vine; you are the branches. If a man remains in me and I in him, he will bear much fruit; apart from me you can do nothing. ⁶If anyone does not remain in me, he is like a branch that is thrown away and withers; such branches are picked up, thrown into the fire and burned. ⁷If you remain in me and my words remain in you, ask whatever you wish, and it will be given you. ⁸This is to my Father's glory, that you bear much fruit, showing yourselves to be my disciples.*

—*John 15:1–8*

GROWTH MUST HAPPEN BEFORE FRUIT IS PRODUCED. AND GROWTH COMES FROM KNOWING HOW TO ABIDE.

Fruitfulness happens in stages and seasons: abide, grow, bear fruit, prune, abide. This is the rhythm of the swinging pendulum, the Semi-Circle. It's really all about timing. We cannot bear fruit if we do not spend time abiding. But we cannot simply stay put in the abide mode, for a branch that does not eventually bear fruit will be cut off and cast into the fire.

It's interesting that nowhere in this text is growth mentioned. Growth seems to be a result of the right rhythm being established. Growth is not the same as bearing fruit. Sometimes we mistake spiritual growth for the fruit itself. This is not the case. We must grow before we can see fruit. An apple tree, for instance, does not bear fruit for three years. Grape vines are pruned back and forced not to bear fruit for two to three years so that their root systems can be established. Growth must happen before fruit is produced. And growth comes from knowing how to abide.

PERMISSION TO BE UNPRODUCTIVE

Let's take a closer look at the first-century process of growing grapes. At the time of Jesus' incarnation, a vine would be cultivated, planted, and left to grow for three years before being allowed to bear fruit. Every time it tried to bring forth a bunch of grapes, it would be cut back. After the third year the grapes would be allowed to grow on their own. By then the branches were strong enough to support the weight of the grapes without breaking. After the harvest, the branches were pruned back for a time of nourishment and rest before the fruit-growing season began again.

Bearing fruit is the most natural thing in the world for a branch.

It doesn't do it by straining to push out a grape. Looking at our lives, however, it would seem producing fruit-making disciples is strenuous. If fruit bearing is not coming naturally in our lives, could it be that we have not spent the proper season abiding? Could it be that we are overgrown branches, too weak to support a single grape, let alone a bunch? Pruning is not the fun part of life. We seldom see churches displaying banners advertising "40 Days of Pruning," or small groups practicing "pruning yourself to a better life." But if a grapevine is not pruned regularly, the branches grow spindly and weak. There is no abiding time when they gain their strength for the growing season.

We need to learn when it is our pruning time. This seems unproductive at first glance. After all, aren't we supposed to be pressing forth with all of our energy to do the work of the kingdom? In a word, *no*. We are supposed to pattern our lives after that of Jesus. (We will look at scriptural examples of the Semi-Circle in the next chapter.) It is not our energy and determination that impresses God, it is our living in the manner he made us that will produce the fruit he intends for us to bear. Pruning is not automatic for the branch. Left to its own plans, it would continue to grow, increasing in size but decreasing in strength, endurance, and health until it would be unable to hold the fruit it is intended to bear.

We need to have times of pruning in our churches, times when most, if not all, activity ceases. Times of rest and abiding. This runs contrary to principles taught in most church growth courses and seminars. How can one grow a church larger by shutting it down for a season? Yet that is exactly what happens at St. Thomas in Sheffield each summer. All small groups come to a stop. Even leadership training goes on hiatus and the worship services are drastically scaled back, so that there is just a simple time of singing and a brief word of encouragement shared. Many of the members go away on holiday or spend more time with friends and family. It looks like nothing is happening. But in this time of abiding, great strength is given to those who do the teaching, singing, and serving throughout the rest of the year. Without a time for their spiritual ground to lie fallow, there would be a very poor harvest in the year to come.

From abiding we grow, from growing we bear fruit, from bearing fruit we are cut back. This is the pattern of the Semi-Circle. When the Lord is moving you into a time of pruning and abiding, surrender to him. There is much grace to be found in the place of abiding.

CHAPTER 8

YOUR PERSONAL STYLE OF REST

*B*efore you begin to practice the rhythm of the Semi-Circle, it is important to discover how you rest. We don't all rest in the same way. Recognizing whether you are an introvert or extrovert is the first step in learning how you rest. Introverts and extroverts are refreshed and energized by different types of rest.

Introverts and extroverts process information differently. For instance, extroverts think by talking. They cannot process information without bouncing their thoughts off another person. They love to talk and brainstorm by thinking out loud. Extroverts are great at ad-libbing, speaking without notes for long periods of time. An extrovert's idea of a relaxing weekend would include entertaining friends, a party, or playing a game with lots of participants.

On the other hand, introverts process information internally. If you pass a new idea by a group of introverts, they will most likely need a day or two to think about it before they can really give you any kind of feedback. They are usually the quiet ones in meetings or small groups as they sit and process what they hear. Introverts are often creative—writers,

WHEN IT COMES TO KNOWING HOW TO REST, UNDERSTANDING HOW GOD HAS CREATED US MAKES ALL THE DIFFERENCE.

> **It took a heart attack and a six-way bypass for me to realize my need for rest. Before my heart attack, I hadn't taken a day off in over two years. God's work was just too important and I had the gerbil syndrome—running as fast as I could even if it didn't get me anywhere. In fact, even after my heart attack, I somehow thought I could heal myself. It wasn't until I had surrendered everything to God—my ministry, my health, my family—that God was able to heal me and I was able to break free of my life of overcommitment. Now I know that I am most effective for God when I make time for silence and solitude. I've found my rhythm of life.**
>
> *— WALT*

painters, composers—who come up with their best art in time spent alone. A restful weekend for an introvert might include pulling the blinds, renting a video or two, and selecting a good book to read.

When it comes to knowing how to rest, understanding how God has created us makes all the difference. If you are an extrovert, don't expect to come away from a quiet evening spent by yourself all refreshed. You will be pining for interaction with others and may actually feel more worn out from being without human contact. Of course, we are to set aside time to spend with the Lord alone. And as we get to know him more intimately, these times will be the most refreshing of all. But there is grace in being who God made us to be. If a cookout with friends is your way to relax, by all means fire up the grill. If you are an introvert, don't feel guilty saying no to the cookout invite. You know that the best way you can relax is to be by yourself for a time. Extreme extroverts and introverts are the farthest points on a continuum, and we are each at different points on the scale. It is important to find your point and discover the best way for you to rest.

Rhythm in Action

God's intention is for us to have rhythm at every level in our lives.

Days

Each day should have structure to enable rest and work, relationships and recreation. We need to work out a healthy pattern that prioritizes our life's circumstances. This framework is the order of our day, our personal disciplines.

Weeks

The seven days of the week give the next level to work out our rhythm. This will involve at least one day for rest and others for work. Our weekly routines should make way for special family members, church, and neighbors God calls us to love as ourselves.

Months

These longer periods give another level to develop variety and contrast— the Semi-Circle in action. Again, a conscious effort is necessary to plan and establish biblical patterns of work and rest so that a dull routine does not take over. Regular times of celebration and retreat should be scheduled so they are not forgotten.

Seasons

These are the phases of a year that enable us to rest for a longer time. Seasons are built into God's creation. We need to build similar seasons into our lives. Seasons include adolescence and adulthood; singleness and

WE ALL NEED TIMES OF EXTENDED RETREAT, RESTING IN THE PRESENCE OF GOD, FOCUSING ON HIM.

marriage; parenthood to empty nest. There is working at a new job or career that may require more of your time than a job you have been at for a number of years. In each of these seasons, you must find time to abide and work.

HOW JESUS RESTED

We can find biblical examples of the Semi-Circle in the lives of many in both the Old and New Testaments. But we want to show LifeShapes from the life of Jesus. He is our compass. And he exhibits the Semi-Circle in his life. If we are to be his disciples, we would do well to follow his example of abiding and fruit bearing. Jesus practiced a rhythm of life. He knew how to order his time in terms of being with his Father and doing the work of the kingdom.

Resting Through Extended Times of Retreat (Mark 1:12–13)

Before Jesus began his ministry, he went out into the desert for forty days where he was tempted by Satan but made strong in the Spirit. He was alone, away from people, spending time with God. He knew exactly what he needed to do. He knew where he needed to start. He spent time retreating with his Father. The very first thing he did before he could begin his ministry was retreat. Jesus came out of the desert full of the Holy Spirit. What does this say to us? We all need times of extended retreat, resting in the presence of God, focusing on him. Like Jesus, at the start of a new ministry or task or phase in our lives, we need to spend concentrated time receiving power and strength from the Father and sifting our motives.

Regular Daily Times of Quiet Resting with the Lord
(Mark 1:35–39)

In this passage we read that Jesus got up early in the morning to go to a solitary place to pray. He was about to begin his second day of ministry and crowds had already gathered, but Jesus got up early to slip away. Before doing anything else, before starting his day, he rested in the presence of his Father and talked with him.

Teaching the Disciples to Rest
(Mark 6:30–32)

When you look at the pattern of life the disciples began to develop, it's clear that Jesus was trying to teach them the same thing. In this passage, the disciples gathered around Jesus, reporting back to him all that they had done after returning from being sent out in Mark 6:7. So many people were coming and going that they didn't have a chance to eat. Jesus told them to follow him to a quiet place where they could rest and eat. All this happened in the midst of what we would call revival. Jesus made rest a priority, and we are to follow his lifestyle.

Other biblical examples of Jesus following the Semi-Circle's pattern of rest and work are as follows:

- Mark 2:13—Jesus is alone at the lake before teaching
- Mark 3:7—Jesus withdraws with his disciples
- Mark 3:13—Jesus goes up the mountainside and calls his disciples
- Mark 4:35—Jesus leaves the crowds by getting into a boat
- Mark 5:1—Jesus at the lake/hillside
- Mark 5:21—Jesus crosses the lake to the other side again
- Mark 6:45–46—Jesus sends his disciples ahead, dismisses the crowd, and goes up a mountain to pray

THE TRIANGLE

THREE DIMENSIONS ARE NECESSARY
FOR US TO LIVE A BALANCED LIFE.
WE FIND THESE DIMENSIONS CLEARLY
EXPLAINED IN THE TRIANGLE.

CHAPTER 9

JESUS AND THE BALANCED LIFE

When Jesus came to the region of Caesarea Philippi, he asked his disciples, "Who do people say the Son of Man is?"

14They replied, "Some say John the Baptist; others say Elijah; and still others, Jeremiah or one of the prophets."

15"But what about you?" he asked. "Who do you say I am?"

—Matthew 16:13–15

Who is Jesus to you? How you answer that question has more to do with the growth of your church than any strategy or plan. Living out the answer in front of those you lead is equally important. The lifestyle of Jesus was thoroughly consistent. His followers could see it operating on a daily basis. As we take up the challenge to become disciples of Jesus—and to train those in our care to do the same—we need to model our lives after the Master.

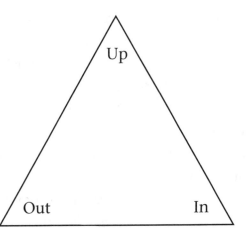

Jesus lived out his life in three relationships: Up—with his Father; In—with his chosen followers; Out—with the hurting world around him.

This three-dimensional pattern for living a balanced life is evident throughout Scripture. It can inform us in how to experience fruitfulness in our ministry, our relationships, and our personal spiritual walk. We see these three dimensions in Jesus' lifestyle throughout the Gospels. Let's take a look at one passage in Luke 6.

JESUS GOT UP

> PRAYER WAS AS FUNDAMENTAL AN ELEMENT IN THE LIFE OF JESUS AS BREATHING. HE INHALED HIS FATHER'S PRESENCE SO HE COULD EXHALE HIS FATHER'S WILL.

12One of those days Jesus went out to a mountainside to pray, and spent the night praying to God.

—Luke 6:12

Jesus prayed regularly. On this occasion he went up the mountain to pray and spent the whole night praying. Mark tells us that when the disciples got up in the early morning, Jesus had already gone out to pray. Luke tells us that he could often be found in lonely places praying. Prayer was as fundamental an element in the life of Jesus as breathing. He inhaled his Father's presence so he could exhale his Father's will.

Jesus was in constant contact with his Father, whom he spoke of in a very personal, intimate, and familiar way. The source of Jesus' fruitfulness was in his Up relationship with the Father. Jesus did what he saw the Father doing. Jesus also introduced his disciples to this very personal relationship with God, calling us into the same kind of intimacy with the Father that he himself has always known. We are to live out the reality of that relationship always.

Our Up relationship with Jesus is how we abide in him. As his disciples, we are to model our life after our Master. We (the branches) must abide in him (the Vine) if we are to produce fruit (John 15). Our efforts are worthless if we do not have the Up in our lives. We will be fruitless without it—there is no other way. ◣

JESUS INVITED OTHERS IN

13*When morning came, he called his disciples to him and chose twelve of them, whom he also designated apostles:* 14*Simon (whom he named Peter), his brother Andrew, James, John, Philip, Bartholomew,* 15*Matthew, Thomas, James son of Alphaeus, Simon who was called the Zealot,* 16*Judas son of James, and Judas Iscariot, who became a traitor.*

—Luke 6:13–16

When Jesus came back from his time of prayer described in Luke 6, he called twelve of his followers to be a "small group." Mark gives us a clearer picture of this group's purpose. "He appointed twelve—designating them apostles—that they might be with him and that he might send them out to preach" (Mark 3:14).

Jesus selected these twelve specifically so he might be with them, spend time with them, and build strong relationships with each of them over the three years he had his public ministry. But this was not just a "seminary setting." Jesus came as a human being and showed us the way human beings are to live out their lives in society with others. From the crowds who followed him, he had seventy-two followers he sent out on kingdom business (Luke 10). From that wider circle, he chose the Twelve, and within

---

◣ FOR MORE ON ABIDING AND FRUITFULNESS, SEE THE SEMI-CIRCLE, CHAPTER 7.

that inner circle, he had three close friends—Peter, James, and John. Jesus shared food with these friends, laughed with them, met their families—in other words, he "did life" with his chosen circle. This was the "In"ward dimension of his relational life.

JESUS REACHED OUT

[17]*He went down with them and stood on a level place. A large crowd of his disciples was there and a great number of people from all over Judea, from Jerusalem, and from the coast of Tyre and Sidon,* [18]*who had come to hear him and to be healed of their diseases. Those troubled by evil spirits were cured,* [19]*and the people all tried to touch him, because power was coming from him and healing them all.*

—Luke 6:17–19

Jesus never lost sight of his Father's vision—to reach out to a dark and dying world. Jesus prayed to his Father before calling a team of people to share in the kingdom work. Jesus chose from the larger crowd of disciples a group who would become his friends, and he lived out his life in their presence. But he also walked among the crowds—teaching, feeding, healing, comforting. Jesus did not wait for the spiritually dead to come to him. He went to them and ministered to them at their point of need—and his critics hated him for it.

> IF WE DO NOT HAVE ALL THREE ELEMENTS OF THE TRIANGLE— THE UP, THE IN, AND THE OUT—WE ARE OUT OF BALANCE, AND WE WILL WOBBLE THROUGH LIFE.

We were created to be three-dimensional beings; when one dimension is missing or is suppressed, the other two do not work as they should. If we do not have all three elements of the Triangle—the Up, the In, and

 FOR MORE ON THIS PRINCIPLE, SEE THE OCTAGON, CHAPTER 23.

the Out—we are out of balance, and we will wobble through life. If you've ever driven a car with tires out of balance, you know what we mean. It's not only a bumpy ride but eventually there will be a blowout—it can be downright dangerous. Jesus' model of a balanced life is also the model needed for a healthy church.

TWO-DIMENSIONAL CHURCHES

Most churches are strong in only two of the three elements—Up, In, and Out. Every church experiences seasons when one or two dimensions receive more emphasis than the others. It is more likely, however, that a church reflects the dimensional strengths of its leadership. So if, as a church leader, you lack balance or you attend to one discipline more than another, it is likely your church will be out of balance as well. But Jesus does not want us to settle for two out of three when his perfect plan is for us to live in balance, with all three dimensions fully functioning. Jesus showed us how and calls us to live in the fullness of three dimensions. Let's take a look at some common two-dimensional types of churches.

Up and Inners

Churches that have traditionally emphasized gifts and the ministry of the Holy Spirit have been very strong torchbearers in the areas of Up and In. These churches have helped to usher in modern worship, with emotionally charged music and introspective lyrics. They have also encouraged conversations with God, talking directly with him as well as listening to his responses. Receiving a "word from God" emphasizes the Up.

These churches also do a good job building community. Small groups based on common interests come naturally in this setting. Bible study (Up)

For my thesis work, I used a story about the two-dimensional inhabitants of a world named Flatland. Flatlanders maintained a simplistic view of life since they could only see everything from the front. Consequently, those living in Flatland had height and length but no depth. The Flatlanders were contented with this limited existence because it was all they had ever known until one day a wind blew across the landscape, lifting one of them up and giving, for the first time, a Flatlander perspective from above. Isn't it amazing how perspective changes everything? Why would any church want to settle for less than the fullness of three-dimensional living?

—MIKE

and fellowship (In) go hand-in-hand in such places. Those on the outside, however, often express how hard it is to be accepted by an established small group. As for the worship itself, people can come and go and remain anonymous. The more exciting and elaborate the worship, the larger the crowd that gathers. And the larger the crowd, the easier it is to attend without commitment. Thus, churches that traditionally stress an emphasis on the gifts and ministries of the Holy Spirit can be said to have strong Up and In relationships, but usually are weak in the area of Out.

Up and Outers

There is another group of churches that is very committed to the Upward aspect of the Triangle. Churches that have traditionally emphasized the importance and inerrancy of the Scriptures have helped to make the Bible available to the widest audience possible through readable translations and practical, expository teaching. From these churches we have also learned much about prayer, as they emphasize the verse "Ask and it will be given to you, seek and you will find" (Matt. 7:7). While the expression looks different than our first group, they have a strong Up dimension.

This group of churches also is concerned about reaching outside the church walls to the surrounding community. Outreach campaigns and witnessing seminars are held regularly in these churches, enabling us to take the Gospel to the lost. You also will find strong global support of mission work, both through significant financial contributions and by supplying missionary workers. People in these churches often spend their vacation time participating in short-term mission trips. Out is a real strength for them.

The Inward area of relationship, though, is not so strong in these churches. It may seem that attendance at a small group Bible study is more duty than desire. Self-sacrifice is rightly emphasized, but it somehow seems to also apply to self as it relates to those who belong to the church. "We" is not as important as "they," so the In is out of balance.

In and Outers

Then there are the churches, many of which are part of older, mainstream denominations, that stress the importance of incarnational ministry. These churches often are found in the heart of our cities, perhaps even the only church within the city limits. They do a wonderful job caring for the hurting and lost, providing levels of help that community agencies cannot. Many people are attracted to these churches as safe havens from the dangerous environment that surrounds them. These churches are very strong in both In and Out relationships.

Like our first two groups of churches, these brothers and sisters also are out of balance in their ministry. The emphasis on our revelatory God is not a strength. Prayer is often rote rather than a personal petition. Scripture reading is part of the service format, but is not often expounded. For these churches, Up is the weak link.

EVALUATING YOUR CHURCH

Take a moment to consider your church. Are you strong in proclaiming the Word, in prayer, in worship? This is your Up relationship. How are you in building community, listening, and responding to the needs of those committed to your church? This is In. Do you take the Gospel outside the walls of your church to the community? This is Out. Using this diagnostic, in which of these three areas is your church the strongest? The weakest? Acknowledging where you are out of balance is the first step toward alignment.

You can do the same when evaluating ministries within your church. Let's say a small group leader comes to you questioning why his small group is not growing. Use the Triangle as a diagnostic tool to discern where there may be a weakness in the small group. Ask the leader to evaluate for you, on a 1–10 scale, how their group is doing in Up. Do they have a regular time of worship? Do they spend time studying Scripture together? Do the same with In. How are they doing listening to one anothers' needs, and then setting about to meet those needs? And then comes Out. On a 1–10 scale, how are they in reaching those outside of their small group? Do they have a way to intentionally share the Gospel? If the group is healthy, they will be above 7 in all three areas. If they come in at 6 or less in any area, time and effort need to be spent in order to bring the group into proper balance.

There is no secret formula to church growth. All healthy churches, small groups, and ministries grow. And to be healthy, you must be in relational balance as pictured in the Triangle: Up-In-Out. It really is that easy.

CHAPTER 10

WHAT'S UP?

With what shall I come before the LORD and bow down before the exalted

God? . . .⁸He has showed you, O man, what is good. And what does the LORD

require of you? To act justly and to love mercy and to walk humbly with your God.

—Micah 6:6, 8

When Jesus calls his disciples, he invites them to walk with him. "Come, follow me" (Mark 1:17). The indication is that Jesus is walking, and we are to walk with him.

Here we have, in one verse, the summation of what is expected of us as followers of Jesus. It is a lifestyle of balance in our relationships: Up, In, and Out.

"Act justly"—Out

"Love mercy"—In

"Walk humbly with your God"—Up

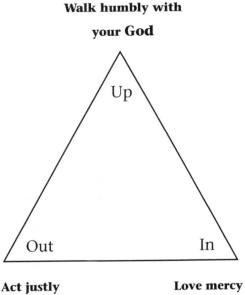

START WALKING

Jesus has invited us to walk with him. This is not just about talking with God. Micah does not read, "*talk* humbly with your God." We have somehow boiled down the Upward dimension of relationship to only talking and listening to God. If our relationships with others, especially those most significant in our lives, were defined only by talking with them, those relationships would be rather limited. The same holds true in our Upward relationship with God. We can't just talk it out—we need to really walk it out with him.

> WALKING WITH JESUS SHOULD BE A JOY, NOT A DUTY.

Walking with Jesus should be a joy, not a duty. Frank Laubach, a missionary to the Moslems of the southern Philippines in the early twentieth century, resolved to pursue the kind of daily intimacy Jesus modeled for his followers. As an ordained minister, he confessed to being ashamed that he had often overlooked the joy of sharing God's presence. His writings encourage us to get to know "the invisible Companion inside you." "God," he wrote, "is infinitely more important than His advice or His gifts; indeed, He, Himself, is the great gift. The most precious privilege in talking with Christ is this intimacy [that] we can have with Him. We may have a glorious succession of heavenly minutes. How foolish we are to lose life's most poignant joy, seeing it may be had while taking a walk alone!"[8]

Walk with Jesus. Invite him to be a part of your everyday life. Let him accompany you as you drive, as you work, as you play. If we are to really be in relationship with him, wouldn't that include our "regular" life as well as those times we set aside as spiritual? Teach your people to be full participants in their own faith journeys as well as the journey you are on together.

THE LOOK OF UP

There was a man in St. Thomas who would go to coffee with Jesus. He pulled up an extra chair to the table. He bought a coffee for himself and two cream cakes—one for himself and one for Jesus. Our friend had only one complaint about spending this time with Jesus. Sometimes, he said, Jesus didn't eat his cake. So, he would have to eat two. Life with Jesus can be just that personal.

—MIKE

We were created to be actively engaged in the Upward dimension of a balanced life. A.W. Tozer expressed it this way: "God formed us for His pleasure, and so formed us that we as well as He can in divine communion enjoy the sweet and mysterious mingling of kindred personalities. He meant us to see Him and live with Him and draw our life from His smile."[9] Can you remember God's smile? If we have not experienced it recently, we may be at a loss to tell others how they can also experience it. How do we do this in our lives? How do you model this with those you are discipling? It would seem that if the chief end of man is to glorify God and enjoy him forever, today's church is spending a disproportionate amount of time on the first half of that statement and giving little attention to the second half.

Many church leaders fall into the trap of being so ministry-focused that they spend too little time enjoying God. Sermon preparation takes the place of delighting in his presence. Prayer is something done mainly for the benefit of others, and the familiarity of worship may not breed contempt but indifference.

We understand completely how that can happen. But we also know that a church without Up is a church lacking in vision and purpose. The good news is that this is not your responsibility alone. As you model this principle and encourage those attending your church to have a walking, talking connection with Christ, as well as balance in the other two dimensions (In and Out), you will find your congregation's unity of purpose and strength of vision increasing.

The Power of Up

> TODAY'S UNCHURCHED ARE NOT SO MUCH REJECTING CHRIST AS THEY ARE SUSPICIOUS OF CHRISTIANS.

Today's unchurched are not so much rejecting Christ as they are suspicious of Christians. Churches that practice the presence of God have great appeal to a generation that is hungrier than ever to know and be known by a God worthy of reverence. Donald Miller, in his book *Blue Like Jazz*, relates the following story illustrating the powerful influence that really knowing Jesus can have.

A guy I know named Alan went around the country asking ministry leaders questions. He went to successful churches and asked the pastors what they were doing, why what they were doing was working. It sounded very boring except for one visit he made to a man named Bill Bright, the president of a big ministry. Alan said he was a big man, full of life, who listened without shifting his eyes. Alan asked a few questions. I don't know what they were, but as a final question he asked Dr. Bright what Jesus meant to him. Alan said Dr. Bright could not answer the question. He said Dr. Bright just started to cry. He sat there in his big chair behind his big desk and wept.

When Alan told that story I wondered what it was like to love Jesus that way. I wondered, quite honestly, if that Bill Bright guy was just nuts or if he really knew Jesus in a personal way, so well that he would cry at the very mention of His name. I knew that I would like to know Jesus like that, with my heart, not just my head. I felt like that would be the key to something.[10]

Like so much of the life of discipleship, the principle of living in intimacy with Christ is both simple and hard. You can invite God into any part of your day. Truth is, he's there already and it is rude to ignore his presence. He's never too busy to talk with you, he enjoys the same things you enjoy, he wants to be a part of your life—he really does.

Chapter 11

Balancing Our In Relationships

One of those days Jesus went out to a mountainside to pray, and spent the night praying to God. 13*When morning came, he called his disciples to him and chose twelve of them.*

—Luke 6:12–13

*J*esus understood the need of every human being for relationship. We long to belong. The need for healthy relationships with other believers in the body, the church, is another aspect of the Inward dimension of the balanced life. It is also part of the training for the sending out of disciples who can make disciples. It is in the In relationship that Jesus modeled the skills his followers would need to grow the church.

As Jesus is our compass, we are to follow his lead in the area of covenantal relationships with one another. Covenant is an underlying principle in Scripture. From the covenant with Abraham in Genesis 15 to the new covenant sealed with the blood of Christ, we are constantly reminded that God has a covenant, or contract, with us. But the idea of covenant is much more than just a contract. It is a gracious commitment, fully identifying with one another, sharing all possessions, loyal no matter the cost. This relationship is expressed in the very nature of God becoming incarnate. This Inward relationship—living in love with one another—is the

THIS INWARD
RELATIONSHIP—
LIVING IN LOVE WITH
ONE ANOTHER—
IS THE ONLY
IDENTIFYING MARK
JESUS SAID
CHRISTIANS WERE
TO HAVE.

only identifying mark Jesus said Christians were to have. "By this all men will know that you are my disciples, if you love one another" (John 13:35).

A CULTURE OF DISCONNECTION

If Jesus, the most brilliant leader of all time, placed a priority on relationships, what can we learn from his example? A healthy relational balance is essential to effective leadership. We were created to be in relationship, to live in society with others. The smallest indivisible unit in the kingdom of God is two. We do not function well when we are left to ourselves. Jesus practiced this principle in his own life, and he taught it to his disciples. He did not send the disciples out alone to do the work he taught them. Even when Jesus sent for a donkey, two disciples were dispatched to lead the animal back. Jesus' followers were not meant to be Lone Rangers. (Even the Masked Man had the faithful Tonto as his partner.)

In our world today, the In relationships are breaking down at ever-increasing rates. We are a nation of fractured families, disenfranchised friends, and increasingly independent individuals. Reality TV lets us experience living life together by proxy. Many faith communities have become little more than gatherings of isolated individuals, while the number of online communities continues to grow. Loneliness has been described as "epidemic." We are a society of disconnected people longing for connections.

WE ARE A SOCIETY
OF DISCONNECTED
PEOPLE LONGING FOR
CONNECTIONS.

You don't have to look far to know this is true. People in your church are in pain because they do not have a strong In aspect in their life. Our culture will continue to try to fill the void if we don't. "The affirming message of the gospel is that God wants to aid and guide us in the struggle to be human and invites us into a relationship with him. The Bible also teaches us that we find ourselves and true fulfillment not in isolation, not even as we engage with one another, but rather when we relate to God through one another. The challenge for the church is to emphasize the communal nature of the Christian faith and to commit to authentic expressions of that nature."[11]

JESUS WASN'T WORRIED ABOUT BEING FAIR

Let's get much more personal here. You can't model for others what you personally are not experiencing. Do you have close friends you can be completely open with? Many pastors make it clear that they are not going to have close relationships with those who attend their church. They may have been burned by someone they had become friends with in the church, and now the scar tissue reminds them to keep a distance. Scar tissue, left unattended, creates complications that lead to great sickness and pain. We need to go to God for healing from wounded relationships, then move on. We cannot stay away from close friendships just because we have been hurt.

Pastors and ministry leaders are sometimes the loneliest people in the church. We have bought into the false idea that we must maintain a professional distance from those in the congregation. Or we want to refrain from "playing favorites." Look once again at Jesus and his relationships. He had three very close friends—Peter, James, and John. What did the other nine think of this? Apparently, Jesus didn't care what they thought. And what did the seventy-two think of the twelve? Jesus had a closer relationship with the twelve than the seventy-two, but again, he doesn't try to be "fair." He needed close friends in his life and did not shy away from inviting the three, then the twelve, into a tighter circle than others. As a leader in your church, you cannot escape the human need for close relationships just because others might be jealous. If you are going to preach the In aspect of life, you need to model it.

JOIN ME, THE KARMA ARMY

In case you think we are carrying this "life together" bit too far, let us tell you about what happened when a single Englishman got an idea.

Danny Wallace was between jobs—having recently left a position as a producer for BBC-TV in London—when he learned his great-uncle, Gallus Breitenmoser, had passed away at the age of ninety. Danny went to Switzerland for the funeral, and while there heard about the crazy idea his great-uncle had pursued.

Following World War II, Gallus had grown tired of living in his city, where there was much gossip and slandering, and wanted to do life with others who would work and live together out of respect for one another. He owned some land, so he decided to start a community farm, hoping to attract one hundred others to live with him.

He got only three.

After a week, he gave it up. But for the rest his life, his family talked about Gallus and his crazy idea. They were still laughing about it at his funeral. This was the first Danny had heard of his great-uncle's quest for community. And the more he thought about it, the more Danny wanted to see if he could collect people together today. In a tribute to Gallus, Danny placed a small ad in a small London newspaper. It read,

> *Join Me. Send one passport-sized photo to . . .*
> (and he gave his address)

A few days later, Danny received a letter from Christian Jones, who included a photo of himself as well as a menu from an Indian restaurant in his part of London. Danny had his first joinee. He put up a web site, and in a short time had 101 joinees, surpassing his great-uncle's goal. Why had people joined? There were no meetings planned, no tasks to accomplish. So far, people had just been asked to send in a photo. That's it. Within weeks, more than one hundred people had done so. They signed up for a group for no other reason than to belong.

Danny was astounded and a bit put out. His joinees now expected him to give meaning to this community. But it *had* no purpose . . . until Danny came up with one. He sent an e-mail where he revealed the plans for the collective. They would be called the Karma Army, in which their purpose was to undertake one random act of kindness every Friday, now to be known as Good Fridays. The Karma Army had its marching orders. A joinee would buy a sandwich and give it to a stranger on a bench. Others bought newspapers and gave them to those sitting in the park. Lunches were bought, groceries were carried, lawns were mowed: all done freely because they were part of the Karma Army.

JoinMeUSA.com is now the Web site where those in the United States can go to become part of the Karma Army. It continues to grow worldwide in spite of the fact that there are no club dues, no regularly scheduled meetings, no rules and regulations to follow. Or, perhaps it is growing because there are none of these things.

People are starving for community. So hungry, in fact, that they will join others simply because they are asked to. Where is the church with this hunger going

PEOPLE ARE STARVING FOR COMMUNITY. SO HUNGRY, IN FACT, THAT THEY WILL JOIN OTHERS SIMPLY BECAUSE THEY ARE ASKED TO.

on around us? Why do we not ask others to join us? Danny Wallace and his Karma Army get it—we must have the In as part of our lives to be balanced and whole. And if Christians are not going to lead the way, then the Karma Army will.

CHAPTER 12

BALANCING OUR OUT REACH

*J*esus lived a three-dimensional life. First, he did nothing apart from his Father. He called a team of people together to be his friends in the kingdom community he was building. Having communicated with the Father (Up) and gathered these friends (In), Jesus then moved (Out) into the crowd and did the work of the kingdom—proclaiming the Good News, challenging injustice, teaching the people, healing the sick, and revealing the love of the Father to the world. Most in your congregation will eagerly practice the Upward dimension of the relationship triangle. They may even be willing to work harder on their relationships within their close circle—the Inward dimension. However, the thought of giving expression to their faith in relationships outside of their comfort zone may be a frightening idea.

One of the most obvious areas of seismic cultural change is in outreach. In the past, nonbelievers clearly identified the church as the place to go for answers to spiritual questions. Many of our current models of evangelism are still based on that premise. Unfortunately, many of these methods are still navigating by landmarks that are no longer there: a shared moral code, childhood exposure to church, a common spiritual language. We continue to offer answers to questions that most unchurched people are no longer asking. Today we have a generation of nonbelievers that might not ever

TODAY WE HAVE A GENERATION OF NONBELIEVERS THAT MIGHT NOT EVER DARKEN THE DOORS OF A CHURCH UNLESS THEY HAVE ALREADY HAD A POSITIVE ENCOUNTER WITH A CHRISTIAN IN THE WORLD.

darken the doors of a church unless they have already had a positive encounter with a Christian in the world.

The idea of evangelism frightens many Christians. They rarely see outreach modeled in a way that they feel capable of doing. That is why their evangelistic efforts are usually confined to bringing a friend or colleague to church in hopes that *you* will share the Gospel with them. But once Jesus' strategy of outward relationships is explained, that fear often vanishes. When they are encouraged to look for people they naturally connect with and build relationships with them, sharing the Gospel message seems much more possible. We don't have to force ourselves on the unsuspecting: we can make a connection with a person God has already prepared.

THE UNCOMFORTABLE BALANCE

Jesus said he would make us fishers of men. In Jesus' day, fishing was done primarily with nets, unlike our recreational method of hook and bait. The men worked cooperatively to lower the nets into the waters, dragging them through the sea toward the boats, where they could be hauled onboard. Dragnet fishing indiscriminately gathered in fish of all sizes, along with a good bit of sea debris. The keen eyes of the fishermen were then set to sort through the catch. It was grueling work but the fishermen never expected the fish (or just the right fish) to jump into their nets. If we simply stay in our safe zones—our church, our small group, our Christian sub-culture—we will not be where the lost are. We have to leave our comfortable settings and get out where there are people who do not yet

FOR MORE ON THIS PRINCIPLE, SEE THE OCTAGON, CHAPTERS 22 AND 23.

know that God loves them so much he cannot stop thinking about them. We must have an outward relational dimension in our lives that draws others in.

LIVING OUT OF PURPOSE

Let's revisit Danny Wallace and his collective known as JoinMe. Within a relatively short time, several thousand joinees sent their photos to Wallace to become part of this collection of diverse individuals from all over the world. Each joinee had an upward relationship with Danny, whether they met him at a pub in London or on his American book tour, or

While I was vicar at Brixton, I was quite successful at getting loads of workers to donate time and money to serve the community. I could have been quite proud of myself if God hadn't one day challenged me to take a look at how our resources were actually being used. Much of what had been given for the community was actually going to people sitting in offices. The next day I asked our entire team to get their coats and follow me outside. We were freezing and everyone's hands were shaking as I handed each one a month's wages in exchange for their keys to the building. "You are here," I told them, "to reach these people and to have a passion for it. I'll take care of the offices and you don't need to show up on Sunday. See you in a month." Some left, but those that rediscovered their mission focus prospered.

—MIKE

only communicated with Danny via e-mail. In any case, there was an active Up element with the creator/vision-keeper. (Note: Individuals who don't know our transcendent God often default to another human to fill the need for the Up relationship.)

Of course, the In dimension was seen in their JoinMe gatherings. Sometimes these were planned events, but most of the time it was just a spontaneous get-together in a pub or coffee shop. New friendships were made between former strangers.

But Join Me would not have lasted had the members not found a purpose, a cause, a way to reach out to those not in their collective. Danny realized this and created the Karma Army. Joinees are all encouraged to sign Good Friday Agreements, promising to carry out at least one random act of kindness to a total stranger every Friday. Danny paints this picture of Good Fridays:

All over the country, little things were happening . . . little moments of joy in towns and cities across the land. Little events that were brightening up people's lives, even if it was for just a few seconds. Pints were being bought for strangers. Shopping was being carried. Cups of tea paid for. Boxes of chocolates handed out in the streets. Flowers deposited at old people's homes. Cakes left on doorsteps. Sure, none of these events was world-changing, but they were . . . well . . . life-affirming, somehow. Strangers being nice to strangers. For no reason whatsoever.

All over Britain, and, in fact, all over Europe now, thousands of people are sticking to their Good Friday agreements and carrying out their little acts of kindness, for no reward or personal gain other than the warm glow they get for having done one. The Karma Army is non-religious. It is non-political. It is about walking into a pub, buying a pint, putting it on a stranger's table with a nod, and walking away. It's about offering someone your [newspaper] on Sunday when you've finished with it. It's not about being thanked, or getting any credit, or going to heaven. It's not about changing humanity; it's about being human.[12]

Danny Wallace and his joinees get it. We do not encourage all the things they do. Yet it seems to us that they are doing what the body of Christ is supposed to be doing. They have seen that life only works when all three dimensions of relationship are present. They have Up, In, and Out all in place in their lives. We are all made to have a relational balance in our lives. Somehow, Join Me has stumbled onto this where many churches today haven't.

> OPERATING IN ALL THREE DIMENSIONS MAY NOT COME NATURALLY, BUT IT IS HOW GOD MADE US TO FUNCTION. IF IT DOES NOT COME NATURALLY, IT MUST BE DONE INTENTIONALLY.

Operating in all three dimensions may not come naturally, but it is how God made us to function. If it does not come naturally; it must be done intentionally. We have to make a commitment and effort to have Up, In, and Out in balance. When one dimension is missing or is suppressed, the other two do not work as they should. Up, In, and Out provide three-dimensional balance in the relationships that make up your life and the life of your church in the same way Jesus modeled for us while here on earth. Our intention should be to live all three dimensions in our lives. When we do, we will experience fruitfulness.

THE SQUARE

THE SQUARE LAYS OUT THE STAGES
EVERY DISCIPLE EXPERIENCES AND
GIVES YOU THE CORRESPONDING
STYLES OF LEADERSHIP.

CHAPTER 13

DEFINING THE PRIORITIES OF LIFE

Jesus called them together and said, "You know that those who are regarded as rulers of the Gentiles lord it over them, and their high officials exercise authority over them. 43Not so with you. Instead, whoever wants to become great among you must be your servant, 44and whoever wants to be first must be slave of all. 45For even the Son of Man did not come to be served, but to serve, and to give his life as a ransom for many."

—Mark 10:42–45

*J*esus' leadership style provides us with powerful tools for leading the church through the current challenges of cultural change. The old adage that "as the leaders go, so goes the church" is true. Leadership "Jesus style" is not about position, as we can see from the passage in Mark 10, but about how we relate to one another. Our priority as leaders should be to live out a transformed life in front of those we seek to lead. To do this, many of us will have to change our leadership style.

MANAGED TO DEATH

Our culture, and as part of it the church, has developed into a management-oriented society. We want to manage growth, manage productivity, and manage human resources. In times of crisis, however, people do not turn to managers for help. In those times, we need leaders. In times of war, soldiers do not follow a manager. In a hospital ER, it takes a leader to make split-second decisions that will save a life. We want off the management-merry-go-round.

That is what the church is crying for today. Dan Kimball puts it this way: "Leadership in the emerging church is no longer about focusing on strategies, core values, mission statements, or church-growth principles. It is about leaders first becoming disciples of Jesus with prayerful, missional hearts that are broken for the emerging culture. All the rest will flow from this, not the other way around."[14]

> I used to feel that a management-driven church was the best leadership style to adopt. I hired staff to oversee various ministries and groups in the church, and I managed the staff. Management is an easier road to follow, because management does not pursue change; it wants to maintain the status quo. But the environment around our church did not stand still. People changed, their needs changed, and the ways to meet those needs changed. Yet we sought to maintain what we had already achieved. The more I managed, the further removed I became from the community of our church. Finally, I realized that I needed to return to leading rather than managing.
>
> —WALT

We need leaders who will step out of "doing church" and lead us to be the church. We need those who are not afraid to dive head-first into our culture with the message of God's unconditional love and his incredible buy-back offer of redemption. But we in the church have failed to train men and women to lead in the style of Jesus. Perhaps we were ignorant. Maybe we are afraid. Whatever the excuse, we now have churches full of managers but lacking in leaders.

For many, a management-oriented pastor feels "safer" than a leadership-oriented pastor. Get things to a good-enough state and keep them that way. That is the safe way, the path that will not take us astray. Yet, as can be attested by the business community, standing still is simply a slow way to die. We need leaders to keep us constantly moving with God.

A SQUARE MODEL FOR LEADERSHIP

There is a great need to restore and encourage leadership in our culture, including the church. And the church is the best place to offer a genuine model of leadership. We have Jesus' example to learn from and to share with the rest of the world. When we take on the lifestyle of Jesus as a leader, those outside the church will see and respond. This is not just a message to senior pastors. We are all called to be leaders, if even of just one other. The commission to go and make disciples is a call for leaders—you are leading when you are making a disciple. A true leader looks like a sheep from the front and a shepherd from behind. Someone is looking for you to lead, and you are looking for someone else to lead you. There is a continuous chain of following the leader in the church and in society. Thus, it is vital for us to distinguish between management and leadership, and answer the call to be leaders.

> A TRUE LEADER LOOKS LIKE A SHEEP FROM THE FRONT AND A SHEPHERD FROM BEHIND.

Jesus was the best leader the world has ever seen. He was also the greatest leadership trainer. If we follow his example and his teachings, we can be the leaders God intends us to be. Jesus' leadership is seen in four stages or phases, thus the use of a Square to discuss leadership. Each side of the Square, or phase of leadership, leads to the next, creating a cyclical process. However, as we examine the four stages of leadership modeled by

Jesus, we also need to understand the four stages of discipleship and how they interrelate with each other.

Stage One

[15]*"The time has come," he said. "The kingdom of God is near. Repent and believe the good news!"*

[16]*As Jesus walked beside the Sea of Galilee, he saw Simon and his brother Andrew casting a net into the lake, for they were fishermen.* [17]*"Come, follow me," Jesus said, "and I will make you fishers of men."* [18]*At once they left their nets and followed him.*

[19]*When he had gone a little farther, he saw James son of Zebedee and his brother John in a boat, preparing their nets.* [20]*Without delay he called them, and they left their father Zebedee in the boat with the hired men and followed him.*

—Mark 1:15–20

This passage describes Jesus' encounter with his first disciples. It doesn't appear that Jesus chooses these guys on the basis of their resumes or their spiritual gift inventories. He simply offers them a relationship with himself and a vision to follow. Their enthusiasm fuels their confidence and immediately they step out, put down their nets, and follow him. They are confident but incompetent—they have no experience to base their confidence on. Are they scared? Probably. Had they known what awaited them on the journey, would any have started? Who can say? Yet into that situation, Jesus speaks clearly and directly, drawing them in.

Jesus is directive and not particularly democratic. He doesn't begin with consensus-style leadership. He doesn't try to get any of these fishermen to agree with his strategy and tactics. He doesn't call for a vote on his teaching of the kingdom. He simply says, "Come, follow me, and I will make you fishers of men." This is very straightforward language. It is not the language he uses later on in his ministry; this is only used at the beginning. He leads by example, going about the land preaching, healing, casting out demons—while the disciples follow along, watching and observing it all.

> OPERATING IN ALL THREE DIMENSIONS MAY NOT COME NATURALLY, BUT IT IS HOW GOD MADE US TO FUNCTION. IF IT DOES NOT COME NATURALLY, IT MUST BE DONE INTENTIONALLY.

Disciple Style

D1—Confident and Incompetent

- High enthusiasm
- High confidence
- Low experience
- Low competence

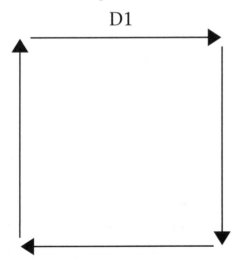

At the outset, if you are a follower, there will be highs and lows. The first stage in development happens when you first encounter a new idea, a new phase, or a new purpose in your life. It could be a new approach to work, a new team at work, a new small group, and so forth. Certain characteristics identify this particular stage. You feel confident and somewhat emboldened because of the new vision that has been shared. Yet you lack competence because you have never had this experience before.

For example, do you remember your first day in college or the first time you preached a sermon? No doubt you were excited—leading to confidence—and felt ready to take on the world. Soon, however, you began to feel the lack of experience and competence. Enthusiasm will only take you so far.

Leadership Style
L1—Directive

- High direction
- High example
- Low consensus
- Low explanation

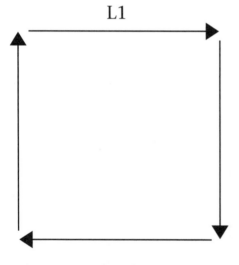

The disciples followed Jesus at the beginning of his ministry as an answer to his call to them. he was directive in his leadership. At the outset of something new, be it a new disciple, new team, new worship service or new task, we should be directive in our leadership. This means announcing a clear direction and walking confidently, not being pushy or unpleasant. The followers are enthusiastic and wanting to do the right thing. Remember, managers do things right while leaders do the right thing. This is a time when an example needs to be set consistently.

This poses a problem for some people. Our system today holds directive leadership to be suspect. We have a legacy within recent memory of directive leaders who have been tyrants, who have manipulated their followers' lives for evil intents. Also, our Western independent mind-set automatically questions directive authority. We live in a democratic society and often think we need to carry this through in everything we do.

Yet when we start out on a new trail, we need a strong, confident leader to show us the way. There will be a time for consensus, for gathering and listening to opinions from those who follow you, but that time is not at the beginning. If you are to lead as Jesus did, you must do so with firmness and confidence. Jesus did not take a vote of his disciples as to where he should go next. He did not commission a survey of the people's felt needs. He started with the kind of confidence and directness we often lack.

> As I got to know Mike's team, I was amazed at how well they all worked together. To me, that is the sign of a good leader, so I asked Mike how he had accomplished it. That's when I was first introduced to the leadership principles of the Square. It all makes so much sense and it is honoring to the people God has chosen for you to lead. It helped me during the process of transitioning our church from the old inherited models and methods of ministry to the new. With so much change happening in the church today, the Square should prove to be an invaluable tool for every pastor.
>
> —WALT

It is imperative to recognize what the beginning of leadership requires. Jesus revealed this in his character and his style of leadership. Are we better leaders than he? Resist the urge to endlessly explain what you are doing or to get feedback from those following. Lay out your plan and stick with it. If people want to follow you, they will. If not, they can get on board somewhere else.

This is why Jesus said that leaders must be broken, humble servants. If

About 1984, an elder from the church I was serving in Brixton came to me and said he had just returned from a leadership conference put on by IBM. He shared with me the four dimensions of leadership as taught at that conference. I searched the Scripture, and saw that Jesus had at least four leadership styles (L1, L2, L3, L4). They went along with the four stages his disciples went through (D1, D2, D3, D4). I began teaching the principles of the Square to my team.

Ten years later, someone came up to me and said, "That sounds like something Ken Blanchard teaches." [13] So I suppose that is where IBM got it. This is how Jesus built his team, and guys today like me and Blanchard and the leaders at IBM are just now catching on. Brilliant, isn't it? I mean, here's teaching that is two thousand years old but perfectly suited for today.

—MIKE

you start out as a directive leader, but are not humble, you will soon find you are walking alone. There are times that a leader must take a stand and walk by himself, but not because of arrogance. Remember that as a leader you are simply a representative of the Good Shepherd.

Stage Two

[32]*"Do not be afraid, little flock, for your Father has been pleased to give you the kingdom.* [33]*Sell your possessions and give to the poor. Provide purses for yourselves that will not wear out, a treasure in heaven that will not be exhausted, where no thief comes near and no moth destroys.* [34]*For where your treasure is, there your heart will be also."*

—Luke 12:32–34

Eventually the disciples become aware that they really have no idea what they are doing. The pressure begins to mount from outside as well as from within—the confidence of these previously successful entrepreneurs hits rock bottom. Worse yet, they suddenly realize they are following a man who is totally opposed by everybody in charge. This man they are following is seen as a curse to leaders of society and the disciples are guilty by association.

The disciples aren't having fun anymore! They start questioning and doubting their call and their decision to follow. We see this in Luke, chapters nine through twelve. At this point Jesus begins saying, "I'll do, but you help." He sends them out to do things he has been doing while they watched: preaching the Gospel, healing the sick, casting out demons. They are laboring in ministry while opposition from the Herodians and the Pharisees increases. The disciples feel overwhelmed; their early confidence is lost and they fall into despair. They fear for their very lives.

Notice that with Jesus' leadership style, experience comes before explanation. He tells the disciples, "Do not be afraid of those who kill the body and after that can do no more. But I will show you whom you should fear: Fear him who, after killing of the body, has power to throw you into hell." They've just had a near-death experience at the hands of the Pharisees. Jesus comes in behind this experience with an explanation of why they do not need to fear these events. He gives them these instructions: "Do not be afraid, little flock, for the Father has been pleased to give you the kingdom. Sell your possessions and give them to the poor. Provide purses for yourselves that will not wear out, a treasure in heaven that will not be exhausted, where no thief comes near and moth destroys. For where your treasure is, there your heart will be also."

> THE KINGDOM OF GOD IS GIVEN, NOT EARNED; RECEIVED, NOT TAKEN.

In essence, Jesus is telling them to let go of their old securities. He wants them to find their security in him. To this point, they probably thought they were going to bring in this kingdom of God. Now they're unsure whether anyone could bring it in. They're scared. Jesus reminds them it is all about grace. It's not what they can do for God, it's what God can do through them.

They need to understand that the kingdom of God is given, not earned; received, not taken. They can't do the work of the kingdom themselves. The kingdom comes only by grace, not works. They began to learn and believe this.

Jesus adapts his directive style of leadership to more of a coaching style, appropriate to this new situation. Key to this is the way he shares his vision and grace with the disciples. He also looks for ways to spend more time with them. He becomes their shepherd, demonstrating the Father's grace and love. They begin going to faraway places just to get away from people. Jesus spends more time alone with his followers in order to relieve their fears and help them focus on what it means to live a kingdom life.

Disciple Style
D2—Unenthusiastic and Incompetent

- Low enthusiasm
- Low confidence
- Low experience
- Low competence

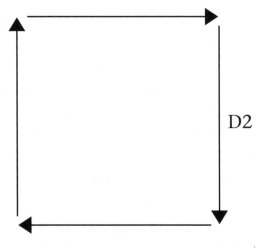

Stage two is the most important in the development process for a disciple. This is when the excitement begins to die down and the feelings of incompetence and inexperience come to the forefront. Disappointments pile up; expectations are not fulfilled. It is hard to realize you really can't do what you are called to do. Opposition and difficulty begin to be overwhelming. You forget the vision and begin questioning how much you really understood it to begin with. There are no highs to balance the lows. You realize you aren't equipped for the mission and soon descend into the deep pit of despair.

Get the picture?

What we tend to do at this point is try to regain the enthusiasm of the D1 stage. Many of us go back and forth from D1 to D2, then D1 and D2 again and again. Instead of allowing God to take us completely through the vulnerability of D2, we want to ignore it and go back to the feelings we had in the D1 phase. But soon we crash back into D2 again. If we do not have a leader to take us through D2, we will bounce back and forth between enthusiasm and despair, with the two coming at ever closer intervals. We must receive the grace that comes only by going all the way through the D2 phase.

Leadership Style
L2—Visionary/Coach

- High direction
- High discussion
- High example
- High accessibility

The second stage is the testing point of any leader. During this stage, the leader should clear his or her schedule and spend time down in the pit with the individual or team going through D2. Leaders

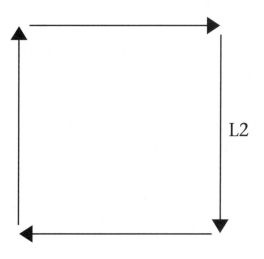

L2

need to be there to offer God's grace and encouragement. The leader at this point can offer a ladder to get out of the pit. The two rungs on this ladder are grace and vision.

It is when a disciple is in the time of discouragement and despair that vision is critical. Vision is needed when you don't know what you are looking at or looking for. Painting a vision for followers does not mean glossing over the hard truth. It simply allows the disciple to say, "Okay—this is what I signed up for. It is about God's kingdom, not my comfort. Let's go."

In this stage the leader needs to talk through the idea of grace, the concept that we can only continue on by God's grace, not by lifting ourselves up by our bootstraps. Grace is an incredibly difficult concept for us as humans to grasp. We all like to think that it's up to us to pull off. It's not up to us—we are simply following God's directions to accomplish his purpose. He will always accomplish what he wants done. It is amazing what happens when a leader can take a person or group out of his own striving and into a place of resting in grace. Their confidence begins to grow because they are seeing it is God's work by grace, not their work by their own effort.

> GRACE IS AN INCREDIBLY DIFFICULT CONCEPT FOR US AS HUMANS TO GRASP. WE ALL LIKE TO THINK THAT IT'S UP TO US TO PULL OFF.

In addition to testing the competence of a true leader, these first two steps are critical to the growth of a disciple. However, the journey and relationship between leader and disciple does not end here; if it does, the leader has failed in his ability to disciple, and the disciple himself will suffer the consequences of being inadequately equipped. As leaders, we must learn to move our disciples, as Jesus did, into a new phase of confidence and experience. ◗

◗ FOR MORE ON PRINCIPLES OF GROWTH, SEE THE HEPTAGON, CHAPTER 20.

CHAPTER 14

THE LANGUAGE OF LEADERSHIP

*T*he goal of spiritual leadership," wrote John Piper, "is to muster people to join God in living for God's glory."[15] To meet this goal, we need to pattern our leadership after Jesus as he mustered his disciples in living for God's glory.

Let's continue our look at how the four stages of discipleship match up with the stages of leadership modeled by Jesus.

Stage Three

[12]*My command is this: Love each other as I have loved you.* [13]*Greater love has no one than this, that he lay down his life for his friends.* [14]*You are my friends if you do what I command.* [15]*I no longer call you servants, because a servant does not know his master's business. Instead, I have called you friends, for everything that I learned from my Father I have made known to you.* [16]*You did not choose me, but I chose you and appointed you to go and bear fruit—fruit that will last. Then the Father will give you whatever you ask in my name.* [17]*This is my command: Love each other.*

—John 15:12-17

Jesus begins to use their time away from the crowds to teach his disciples. This produces in them a renewed confidence based on experience.

A FRIEND IS ONE
WHO EMBRACES A
COMMON OBJECTIVE
AND AIM, ONE WITH
WHOM LIFE IS
SHARED.

In this phase we see a period of growth. This is a time marked by "You do it, I'll help." Jesus did not begin his ministry by calling the disciples with this kind of message, because it would not have motivated them to follow. They needed to go through the pressures, discouragements, and threats until they reached their low point. Once there, they would cleave to Jesus and to one another. There would be consensus.

Jesus now says to them, "You are my friends." Until now, the disciples had been like hired hands, doing what they were told without really seeing the big picture. But now they were called Jesus' friends. A friend is one who embraces a common objective and aim, one with whom life is shared. At this point, relationships begin to get warm. They have communion together. They laugh more. It feels very different from phases one and two. They love to hang out together, share the workload, linger after teaching sessions to discuss what they have heard and what it means. During this phase, Jesus has all the time in the world for them.

Then he drops a bombshell. He tells the disciples he will be leaving them soon. He says he is going to prepare a place for them in the Father's house, and that they know how to get to where he is going. The disciples are confused. Thomas speaks for them all and says, "We don't know where you are going, so how could we know the way?" Jesus answers with perhaps the defining statement of all of mankind's existence: "I am the way, the truth and the life." But they still don't get it. They are happy where they are and don't want this wonderful time to end. All that pain and suffering, and now this. The disciples thought they had endured the hard times and had arrived. It could even be said they were overconfident.

For instance, James and John, the sons of Zebedee, ask to sit to the right and left of Jesus in his glory (Mark 10:37). They have a lot to learn about servant leadership, hence Jesus' response, "Whoever wants to become great among you must be your servant, and whoever wants to be first, must be slave to all" (Mark 10:43–44). James and John are thinking of where they will sit in the kingdom; they believe they have arrived. Jesus talking about going away doesn't fit this scenario. Jesus, though, is preparing them for the final phases.

Disciple Style
D3—Growing Confidence

- Increasing enthusiasm
- Growing experience
- Intermittent confidence
- Growing competence

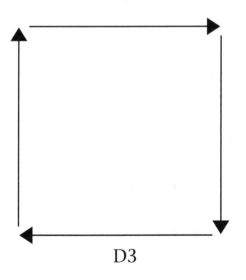

D3

When disciples are in stage three, the concept that sets them free is "God is in charge." They have to acknowledge grace and begin to work it into their lifestyle. This is not easy for most of us, but it is the one thing that will move us on to growth and maturity. It is the one thing that will move us out of the childish ways that blow us in every wind of doctrine, that lead us to grasp at any new thing that comes along. Going to this conference, buying that new book, listening to a new tape, jumping around from church to church—all can be substitutes for growing into the disciples God intends for us to be. We can escape out of that trap and move into a gradual growing process as the Lord works his grace into our hearts. As we walk out the lessons learned in stage two, we once again grow in confidence and find that our enthusiasm is increasing. Because we are beginning to act on what we have learned, we have more experience, and this also helps our confidence and enthusiasm.

At this stage the disciples were spending a lot of time with Jesus. Growth and development as a person is mirrored by a growth in intimacy. There is a growing intimacy between those being led as well as between the follower and the leader.

Leadership Style
L3—Pastoral/Consensus

- Lower direction
- Higher consensus
- High discussion
- High accessibility

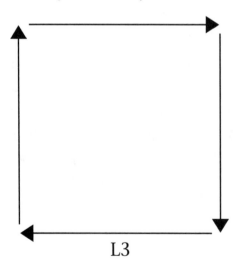

L3

In stage three, strong friendships have been formed between the leader and those he or she is leading. Time spent with the disciples has helped create an intimacy they had not previously felt with Jesus. He calls them his friends at this stage. This is the kingdom in action.

But as soon as this phase gets underway, and the disciples feel that all is well in the world, Jesus starts talking about leaving them. The disciples don't want this to happen. They begin flirting with D2 again. This will most likely happen with those you are leading. Yet you must now trust that your followers have the vision; they know the direction they are to be going.

> IF YOU GIVE DECISION-MAKING ABILITY TO A DISCIPLE TOO SOON, BOTH THE LEADER AND THE FOLLOWER WILL SOON BE OFF TRACK.

You as leader have changed dramatically from a directive style to gathering consensus. Many leaders make the mistake of starting in this phase, trying to have a democratic style from the beginning. This will not work. The followers have to pass through stages one and two before they have the experience and vision to make their opinions worth considering. If you give decision-making ability to a disciple too soon, both the leader and the follower will soon be off track. Each phase must be allowed to run its full course.

Stage Four

18*Then Jesus came to them and said, "All authority in heaven and on earth has been given to me.* 19*Therefore go and make disciples of all nations, baptizing them in the name of the Father and of the Son and of the Holy Spirit,* 20*and teaching them to obey everything I have commanded you. And surely I am with you always, to the very end of the age."*

—Matthew 28:18–20

Sure enough, Jesus is taken away. He is arrested, tried, crucified. He comes back again, yes, but this time as the resurrected Lord. In his resurrected state, he doesn't hang around with them all the time like he did before. He just turns up every so often and in the most surprising ways. They have all the doors and windows locked and all of a sudden Jesus is there. They are scared and Jesus says, "The next time we meet will be in Galilee." So they all go off to Galilee. They search and look, but no Jesus. Not knowing what to do next, they go back to the only other thing they do know: fishing. In the morning, after a fruitless night of not catching fish, they see someone on the beach. Guess who it is?

Jesus is preparing the disciples to spend less time with him. He is reducing their hours of contact with him because he is now delegating authority. He is giving them the job he had done; they are to become his representatives. In this last phase they are now empowered with confidence and competence as a result of their deeper relationship and ministry experience with Jesus.

So we have seen from the very first phase where Jesus says, "Come, follow me" to the last stage where he says, "Go out into all the world and do what I have taught you to do." As the disciples grow and change through each stage, so his leadership style adjusts accordingly. He has taken them through a process of development to equip them for their new task—taking the Gospel into the world.

Disciple Style

D4—The End Is in Sight

- High enthusiasm
- High confidence
- High experience
- High competence

When this stage is reached, the high enthusiasm is not just froth-and-bubble

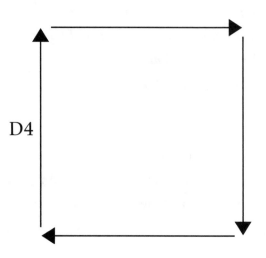

excitement. It has deep roots in confidence, brought about by a strong feeling of competence. There is knowledge of God's Word and his grace. The continual hearing of Jesus' teaching and putting it into practice sends roots down deep, strengthening the disciples against life's inevitable storms. Their confidence is in God, not themselves. They no longer rely on themselves; they trust God to complete what he starts. At this point, Jesus says, "Go and do what I have done—make disciples like I have."

Leadership Style
L4—Delegation

- Low direction
- High consensus
- Low example
- High explanation

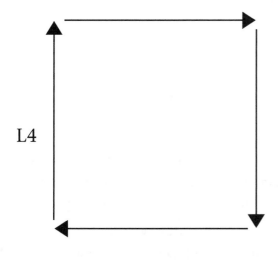

Growth has taken place through the third stage, experience has been gained, and confidence that once was lost now has begun to return. The team now has competence. The leader takes into account what the team thinks and seeks to build consensus. The leader is also lower on example, because at this stage the disciples should be doing the work.

It is now time for delegating authority and responsibility. Good leaders always get people to the stage where they are ready to accept delegated responsibility. Delegating to disciples before this stage is a recipe for disaster. They may think they are ready, but until they have been completely through the first three stages, they are not.

> LEADERS MUST ALWAYS BE LOOKING TO GIVE AWAY THEIR JOBS TO PEOPLE WHO CAN DO IT AS WELL OR BETTER THAN THEY.

Leaders must always be looking to give away their jobs to people who can do it as well or better than they. This calls for a level of intimacy between the leader and disciple that does not last. The leader begins to disengage; the disciple now becomes a leader. The closeness remains and is no longer defined by the amount of time spent together but by the openness with one another.

Stages of delegating responsibility:

- Stage One—I do, you watch
- Stage Two—I do, you help
- Stage Three—You do, I help
- Stage Four—You do, I watch

LOOK DEEPER

Aside from the Scriptures we have looked at in our discussion of the Square, there are many other examples in the Bible of these principles of discipleship and leadership being lived out. For instance, look at the relationship between Mordecai and Esther. In this book, Esther grows in wisdom and maturity as the story unfolds, and by the end is able to make important decisions and take initiative, whereas at the beginning she was heavily dependent on Mordecai as her mentor.

As a leader, it is your responsibility to look inward on yourself and on your capacity to put these principles into practice. Do not be afraid to observe how Jesus and others great leaders of the Bible exemplified the characteristics of the Square and compare that to your own discipleship abilities. By taking an honest look at yourself, you can begin to take the steps necessary in building that same leadership character toward your disciples that Christ showed toward his.

THE PENTAGON

THE PENTAGON IS A TOOL FOR ENABLING EVERY
BELIEVER TO RECOGNIZE HIS OR HER WORTH AND
HOW TO CONTRIBUTE TO THE BUILDING UP OF
THE BODY OF CHRIST.

CHAPTER 15

WHO DOES YOUR CHURCH
BELONG TO?

*T*he cultural shifts of the last several decades have affected the church in another way. More and more church members have turned to the church as a purveyor of goods and services, and the burden of their increasing demands has fallen primarily on the pastor. Leading a church can become such a heavy burden that many pastors leave their churches and forsake their calling. While the Bible clearly defines roles within the church, the mission of the church was intended to be shared by the whole body. A healthy church equips every member to participate in the missional work to which God has called us.

This next shape—the Pentagon—may at first feel threatening to some pastors and leaders because it will require a change in thinking about who your church really belongs to. Church leadership based on high control is not at all attractive to the emerging generation. For the next generation, the journey of faith in community will not be about *doing* church but about *being* the church. Sally Morgenthaler warns, "If we can't live the sacred journey with Christ daily and are not actively drawing others into that journey—way outside the worship center or sanctuary and outside our stained-glass or silk-plant ghettos—we can't expect to do it in an hour on Sunday morning or Wednesday night."[16]

The Pentagon can be great news to you and your ministry. It may feel a

Roger is the senior pastor of a church of nearly a thousand members. He was among a small group of pastors listening to me share about the Pentagon. When I finished, these pastors were asked if they felt threatened by what I had just taught. Roger smiled and shook his head.

"If I apply what you have just shared," he said, "it can be very liberating. It means my staff and I don't have to feel as if it is all up to us. This is great news." We think so, too.

—MIKE

little strange at first, but give it a chance—it will soon feel very comfortable because it is about unleashing the members of the body to function at their full potential. When we know what we have been designed for and called to do, we can save ourselves a lot of effort and striving in areas we were not built for. If we know who God has made us to be, we can stop trying to be someone we are not and let go of the stress that comes with living that kind of life. When we are walking the path God has called us to walk, we will discover grace beyond our expectations to succeed. God has buckets full of grace to pour out on us—but we have to be standing where the downpour is occurring. And that place is where He has designed us to fit.

Many people say to God, "Give me an anointing for this task I am about to undertake." But if this is not the gifting God has given them, there will be no anointing of grace. And without the anointing, there will be no long-term success.

IF WE KNOW WHO GOD HAS MADE US TO BE, WE CAN STOP TRYING TO BE SOMEONE WE ARE NOT AND LET GO OF THE STRESS THAT COMES WITH LIVING THAT KIND OF LIFE.

Think of a person who struggles with math in school. He forces himself to pay attention to the teacher, and just doesn't get it when formulas are explained. His homework constantly has to be reworked, and if he gets a correct answer on a quiz, it is most likely to have been a guess. Now, how would this person fare as an engineer? Would he do good work? Would he even enjoy the job?

If you strive and struggle in a particular area of ministry and find it produces more stress than fruit, perhaps it's time to step back and examine your gifts. Discovering and acknowledging who God has made you to be will ensure you are standing under the bucket of grace, not beside it, and that you get a healthy soaking of grace, not just a splash.

A SPIRITUAL GIFT IS NOT YOUR MINISTRY

Several New Testament passages speak of gifts for the church, including 1 Corinthians 12, Romans 12, 1 Peter 4, and Ephesians 4. Most of us have been taught that God has given us one or several of the gifts listed in these passages, that these gifts are "ours." There is, however, an important distinction between spiritual gifts and roles as mentioned in Scripture. A spiritual gift is not a ministry in itself. Rather, it is a tool to use for the job at hand. The job is the role or function one is called to. To help in differentiating the gifts from a specific role, it is important to look at the context in which each of these passages was written.

I found this new twist on the biblical passage in Ephesians 4 to be very freeing. Like most pastors I had been trying to fill a position that I thought required me to fill all the roles at once. When I discovered that my base was evangelist not pastor, I was actually relieved. It made so much sense once I thought about it. Now I choose to appoint people in the team to complement each other in all five areas of ministry. By concentrating on who God made me to be and helping others do the same, our ministry is much more effective and enjoyable.

—*WALT*

Both 1 Corinthians 12 and Romans 12 contain a list of gifts. What is often overlooked is that Paul wrote each of these letters to different churches facing different problems. He wrote to each of these bodies to teach them about grace and how to apply it to their particular situations.

Paul wrote 1 Corinthians to address problems and issues arising from this church's gatherings. Paul was teaching the Corinthians what their corporate worship should look like. In chapter 12 he explains that they should expect the Holy Spirit to be present in power, and to do certain things. The key word to understanding how the Holy Spirit works is "manifestation" in verse 7. In Greek, the word is *phanerosis*, meaning the revelation or enlightening that God brings. The English word we use for this has its roots in the Latin for "the dancing hand." Isn't that great? The dancing hand of the Holy Spirit falls on certain individuals during a gathering, causing them to exercise one or more of the gifts—wisdom, words of knowledge, tongues, prophecy, and so on. Anyone can receive any of the manifestations, or the dancing hand, of the Spirit mentioned in 1 Corinthians 12. Paul was saying that in corporate worship the Spirit will fall on certain individuals, giving them gifts for the moment. These are not permanent roles; we do not possess these gifts as our own "ministry." The key to the gifts is the Spirit moving as a dancing hand within our gathering, dispensing grace as it is needed.

Similarly, Romans 12 must be examined within the context it was intended. Paul was trying to help the church in Rome get past the growing rivalry and division that existed between Jews and Gentiles. The church was struggling with ethnic division and, thus, not functioning as a single, united church. Paul pleads with them, in view of everything he has shown them about God's mercy and grace, to live sacrificial lives. He wants them to stop arguing and start living their lives for one another. Sacrifice and service are the context of this passage. Paul gives some practical examples: If your gift is teaching, stick to teaching. If it is to give aid to those in need, keep your eyes peeled for opportunities. This is not meant to be an exhaustive list of roles within the church, merely a few examples used to make a point.

Both Romans and 1 Corinthians were written to specific churches facing specific problems and circumstances. The Book of Ephesians, though, was not written to just one church for a special moment in time, but for the all the churches in the region of Asia Minor. Ephesians is a memo of sorts to many churches. It doesn't address specific problems but outlines foundational teachings for how a church should function. In it, Paul shares what the roles of all believers are to be within the church.

THE FIVEFOLD MINISTRIES ARE FOR EVERYONE

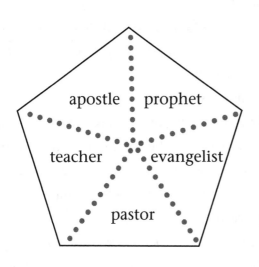

"But to each one of us grace has been given as Christ apportioned it . . . It was he who gave some to be apostles, some to be prophets, some to be evangelists, and some to be pastors and teachers, to prepare God's people for works of service, so that the body of Christ may be built up until we all reach unity in the faith and in the knowledge of the Son of God and become mature, attaining to the whole measure of the fullness of Christ" (Eph. 4:7, 11–13).

"But to each one of us . . ." It has been a traditional teaching that the fivefold ministries in this passage are five roles for leaders in the church. But that

is not what the verse says. "To each one" refers to every
member of the church, not just leaders. What the Bible
says is that each one of us has received a portion of grace
in one of five roles. That grace has come to us in the
form of a call to be one of five types of people. There is
no mention of leadership in this passage, so we can see

> "TO EACH ONE"
> REFERS TO EVERY
> MEMBER OF THE
> CHURCH, NOT JUST
> LEADERS.

that this is not just for those who have been ordained or
have been through seminary. The fivefold ministries in Ephesians 4 are for
"each one of us."

". . . grace has been given as Christ apportioned it." The fivefold roles apply
to all members of the body of Christ in varying degrees. What Paul is saying
is that Jesus, by the gift of his grace, has empowered and equipped each of
us for service. We have all been given different-sized portions of grace and
anointing. We each receive part of the whole. Christ's ministry fully demonstrates all five roles of apostle, prophet, evangelist, pastor, and teacher. We as
members in his body receive one of these five appointments, relying on one
another for those areas we are not gifted in.

*"It was he who gave some to be apostles, some to be prophets, some to be evan-
gelists, and some to be pastors and teachers, to prepare God's people for works of
service so that the body of Christ may be built up."* These five gifts of grace seem
to be the elements needed for preparing people for service and building up
the church. Each person receives a portion of grace to fulfill a ministry role
as an apostle, prophet, evangelist, pastor, or teacher.

*"Until we all reach unity in the faith and in the knowledge of the Son of God
and become mature, attaining to the measure of the fullness of Christ."* When
each person is working, by grace, in the role given by the Holy Spirit, the

result is unity in faith, a continual growing in the personal knowledge of Jesus, and maturity or wholeness, which all lead to the fullness of Christ.

When looking at each part of the passage in context, it becomes clear that the gifts mentioned in Ephesians 4 are roles or functions given to each believer, and that the gifts mentioned in 1 Corinthians and Romans are tools to enable every believer to function more effectively in his or her role.

When all the roles of apostle, prophet, evangelist, pastor, and teacher are operating effectively within a church, then all the people are being prepared for service and are being built up. The results will be unity, knowledge of Christ, spiritual maturity, and the fullness of Christ. What a great picture of how the church should look. How liberating for you, a leader within the church, to know that you do not have to do it all. God has called everyone to take a part in his body.

> HOW LIBERATING FOR YOU, A LEADER WITHIN THE CHURCH, TO KNOW THAT YOU DO NOT HAVE TO DO IT ALL.

He will always accomplish what he wants done. It is amazing what happens when a leader can take a person or group out of his own striving and into a place of resting in grace. Their confidence begins to grow because they are seeing it is God's work by grace, not their work by their own effort. By knowing how to identify the roles of the Pentagon and how and by whom they are being filled within your church, your small group, or your ministry, you can implement a process in which all of these people can learn to work effectively and productively together in ministry. As they (and you) begin to understand their place in God's plan, they will begin to rest in the confidence of God's grace.

CHAPTER 16

THE FIVEFOLD FOUNDATION FOR MINISTRY

*L*et us look in more detail at each of the five roles as we see them in Ephesians 4. Then we will help you to know what your base and your phase ministries are and how best to utilize them.

APOSTLE

From the Greek *apostolos* meaning "one who is sent out." Apostles are visionary and pioneering, always pushing into new territory. They like to establish new churches or ministries. They come up with new, innovative means to do kingdom work.

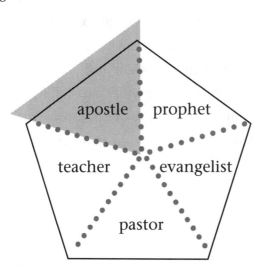

- Biblical examples—the Twelve, Paul, Priscilla, and Aquilla.
- Jesus' example—Jesus was the one sent by God (John 3:16).
- Apostles enjoy dreaming, doing new and challenging tasks, change.
- Secular examples—entrepreneurs, explorers.

PROPHET

One who hears and listens to God (*prophetes*); the prophet foretells and tells forth revelation from God. Often they are able to stand back from circumstances to get a clear picture of what is happening and therefore see creative solutions and develop a vision for situations others don't see. They understand the times and what people should do.

- Biblical examples—Anna and Simeon in Luke 2 as they prophesy over the infant Jesus. Agabus in Acts 11:28 and 21:10 when he predicts a famine and prophesies about Paul. Philip's daughters in Acts 21:9 were all known as prophetesses.
- Jesus' example—Every word spoken from the mouth of Jesus was revelation from God. He often foretold events such as Peter's denial and the details of his own death. He, himself, is the fulfillment of Old Testament prophecy concerning the Messiah such as found in Isaiah 53.
- Prophets enjoy being alone with God, waiting, listening.
- Secular examples—people who speak out their perceptions. They're often creative types, musicians, and artists.

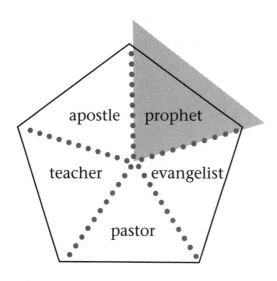

EVANGELIST

One who brings good news and shares the message readily (*euanggelistes*). Evangelists love spending time with non-Christians and often remind other Christians that there are non-Christians still out there in the world. They are not necessarily all like Billy Graham; they may be "people gatherers." Evangelists know the Word and can make it relevant to non-Christians.

- Biblical example—Philip in Acts 8:12. The people believed Philip when he preached.
- Jesus' example—Jesus embodied the Good News. He *was* the Good News. We can see Jesus as evangelist in John 3 with the Samaritan woman at the well.
- Evangelists enjoy discussion and sharing their point of view.

Wherever they go, they seem to draw others into discussion about Jesus. They are passionate about sharing the Gospel. They are not timid about their faith and seem to easily share with others regularly.

- Secular examples—salesmen, politicians, public relations reps.

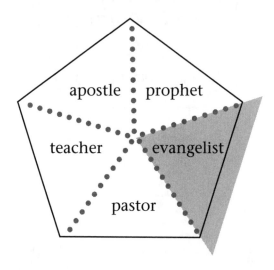

PASTOR

One who shepherds God's people (*poimen*), who cares for others with a tender heart. One who sees needs, provides comfort, and encourages others. Pastors spend most of their time with other Christians. They can easily empathize with others and exhibit lots of patience with those in need.

- Biblical example—Barnabas in Acts 15:36–41. Barnabas clearly demonstrates a pastoral heart in his defense of Mark.

- Jesus' example—In John 10, Jesus refers to himself as the Good Shepherd who has come to lead his people.
- Pastors enjoy one-on-one chats and showing hospitality. They get burdened by others' problems and have a knack for speaking the truth in love. They are good listeners and are easy to talk to and share inner feelings with.
- Secular examples—counselors, social workers, nurses, and anyone in the care-giving professions.

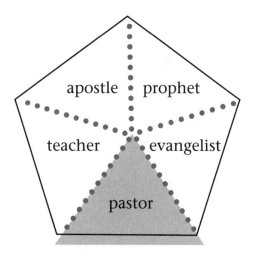

TEACHER

One who holds forth the truth and is excited by it (*didaskalos*). The teacher looks for ways to explain, enlighten, and apply truth.

- Biblical example—Apollos in Acts 18.
- Jesus' example—He was often referred to as Teacher or Rabbi. His "students" often remarked that his teaching was different because he taught with authority.

- Teachers enjoy reading and studying the Bible and helping others to understand it.
- Secular examples—lecturers, trainers, school teachers.

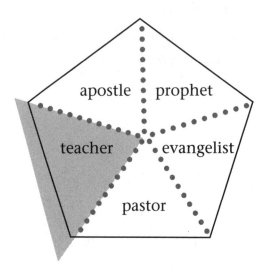

BASE AND PHASE

Each of us has a base ministry that represents one of the fivefold ministries in Ephesians. We believe that God gives each of us this ministry and it is ours for life. Hence we call this our "base ministry." But there are also particular periods when God leads us to discover and understand the other ministries for a brief time. This is what we call our "phase ministries." We all have our base and at least one phase ministry at any given time.

For example, the Lord may call you to go on a short-term mission trip (evangelist) or teach an Alpha course (teacher), but these may not necessarily be the ministries that you feel most comfortable with. Your base ministry will be the one that refreshes you, the one you are most passionate about. The Lord, however, will mature you by taking you through each of the other ministries in phases. It has been the experience of many that the Lord will make your base ministry more rounded as you

THE LORD WILL MAKE YOUR BASE MINISTRY MORE ROUNDED AS YOU EXPERIENCE PHASES IN THE OTHER AREAS.

experience phases in the other areas. What God seems to be doing by allowing you time in the phase ministries is to strengthen your base ministry.

To give another example, the Lord may give you a vision and grace for initiating a new ministry within your church that requires you to be more apostolic. Your base ministry, however, is as a teacher. You are invigorated by the new challenge and stretched as you trust the Lord to see you through, but eventually the stress of operating outside of your base will cause you to want to return to the area you really love and are energized by doing.

A warning: It is easy to fall into the trap of feeling as though you need to excel in all five ministries all the time. But this only leads to burnout and a failure to focus properly on your base ministry. Worse still, you will not be making room for others around you to explore their base ministries.

What happens when grace for your phase ministry has been used up and it's time to return to your base? Generally you will know you have run out of grace. Energy and enthusiasm dry up. You see less blessing and less fruit from your efforts, even though you are working at the same intensity level. Eventually you will experience less peace about what you are doing. This naturally leads you to less joy at the task. Your thoughts turn to doing what you really love and what comes naturally for you. Going back to your base

WE ARE THE BODY OF CHRIST, WHICH MEANS THAT TOGETHER, WE REPRESENT THE MINISTRY OF JESUS WHO WAS THE EMBODIMENT OF ALL FIVE MINISTRIES IN EPHESIANS 4.

ministry is the only thing that gives you a sense of peace.

We are not all called to be pastors, but we are all called to care. We are not all called to be teachers, but we are all called to hold out the Truth. We are all responsible for learning how to listen for God's voice, something that comes more naturally for the prophet. We are all called to share the Good News with others, but this takes all those who are not called to be evangelists out of their comfort zones. And we are not all apostolic, but must all learn to walk out into what God calls us to do. We are the body of Christ, which means that together, we represent the ministry of Jesus who was the embodiment of all five ministries in Ephesians 4. He is the perfect presentation of the ministry of the Spirit. By experiencing all five areas of ministry, whether as a base or a phase, we grow more into the likeness and character of our Master.

CHAPTER 17

DISCERNING YOUR CORE CALLING

Once you have explained that every member of the body is equipped with one of the fivefold ministries as a base, the first question that will arise will be, "How do I know what my base gift is?" We are including a tool to help determine one's base gift in the Appendix. Feel free to use this as you like; it is but one way to determine one's gifting. In the end only God can confirm a calling. Looking at our personality type is a major indicator of the gifting he has placed within us.

HOW TO FIND YOUR BASE

Take a look at your own personality—a true, honest look. Are you an introvert or an extrovert? This has nothing to do with how confident you feel. Being an introvert does not equal lacking confidence. And not all extroverts feel confident all the time, even though they may appear so on the outside. Being an introvert or extrovert has to do with the way you function and process information. It can also indicate your base ministry gift.

Extroverts think by talking things through with others. Being in the company of others and participating in group activities refreshes an extrovert. The extrovert tends to work well with things that are immediate and can be seen quickly. They can ad-lib easily. Extroverted preachers can speak off the cuff. For the most part, it seems most apostles, prophets, and evangelists are more extroverted.

Introverts think by internally processing things. An introvert is refreshed and recharged by reflection and spending time alone. Introverts are usually very creative. Some of the great writers, painters, and composers have been introverts. Introverted preachers feel much more comfortable when they have their entire sermon written out and displayed in front of them. Pastors and teachers tend to be introverted.

This is not, of course, a clear-cut way to define one's ministry. There are many who fall in the middle of the continuum between introvert and extrovert. There is another measuring device, determining if one is a pioneer or a settler, that may help you narrow your options.

ARE YOU A PIONEER OR A SETTLER?

Your reaction to or excitement over a new project or task can shed light on your base gifting. We call the two far points on this scale "pioneer" and "settler." Pioneers, for example, enjoy change and find the stress of doing new things exciting rather than threatening. They are committed to flexibility; instability does not frighten them. They reach out beyond their current experiences and relationships to discover new frontiers and challenges. They often find themselves bored and frustrated by the discipline necessary to sustain what has been established. They love to make breakthroughs and are always looking for the next frontier to explore and tame.

Settlers are committed to continuity, stability, and conservation. They prefer to grow and develop plans rather than scrap what they have and start

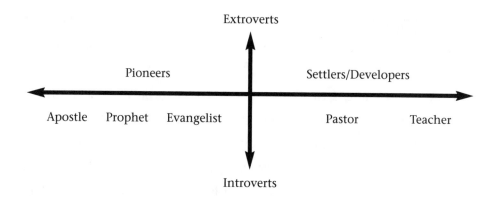

over with something brand new. They are great at implantation and processing; they like to see things through to the end. Settlers are the steady, solid backbone of most communities. They like to know what to expect, and they feel most comfortable when things are moving smoothly according to plan. Instability causes great discomfort for settlers.

All through history there has been interplay between pioneers and settlers. A look at American history reveals a continuing balance between those who go forth to explore new territory and those who follow to build houses, stores, schools, and churches in these newfound places. The two do not always exist well together. The pioneer gets bored and restless if asked to stick around to help paint and decorate the buildings once they are up, and the settler is uneasy at the thought of going to live in the wilderness without the comforts of home.

Both pioneers and settlers, however, are vital. Without the pioneers we will never find the next frontier. We will not reach beyond what we have already achieved. Pioneers are always looking beyond what we have already received to what lies ahead. Without the settlers, we would never keep the frontier that was won by the pioneers. The pioneers will have pushed on to new territory, leaving the recently discovered land barren. Settlers must come to build and occupy, to maintain and to increase through steady, deliberate efforts.

Pioneers look ahead to the frontier and seek to break new ground by putting visionary ideas into practice. Settlers consolidate the frontier that has been won by the pioneer and play an important role in the continued health of the land. In church terms—generally speaking—the pioneers would be the apostles, prophets, and evangelists. Pastors and teachers tend to be of the settler nature.

The church needs both pioneers and settlers, yet the tension between the two must be understood and managed to keep from being swallowed by division. Pioneers naturally want to move into new ways and ideas to advance the kingdom. They are willing to take risks to join the Lord in new endeavors, often long before the settler even knows the Lord is moving in that direction. Off goes the pioneer, with excitement that cannot be contained but that disturbs the settler who is working to preserve what has been handed down by previous generations. "It worked for them, so it will work for us" is the settler's life motto. Settlers look to put down roots while pioneers are hacking through dense jungle growth in the search for new territory. Many churches split, not because of theology, but because they don't understand the interplay between pioneers and settlers.

MANY CHURCHES SPLIT, NOT BECAUSE OF THEOLOGY, BUT BECAUSE THEY DON'T UNDERSTAND THE INTERPLAY BETWEEN PIONEERS AND SETTLERS.

In some churches, the pioneers are driven away by settlers who do not want to explore anything new. In others there is pain caused by pioneers who are not patient enough to wait for settlers to catch up with them. There needs to be a mutual respect and acceptance, for without both pioneers and settlers the kingdom will not grow.

The Continuum . . . Get Flexible

When we speak of pioneers and settlers, of introverts and extroverts, we are not referring to rigid categories. This is not black and white. Each person falls at a point on the continuum between the two extremes, and can even move back and forth between the two. Different situations and circumstances draw us up and down the line. Those who handle stress and pressure the best are those who move most freely over the greatest distance on the pioneer/settler continuum.

> God stretches us by taking us into the territory we do not naturally feel comfortable in.

Testing comes into our lives to make us more flexible, to stretch us out of our comfort zone. God stretches us by taking us into the territory we do not naturally feel comfortable in. When we move in a direction that is not our natural reaction (a pioneer acting as a settler, for instance), it brings about maturity. We do not grow by staying in our comfort zone. It is by moving toward the other side of the continuum that we experience growth and maturity. Once this period of testing is over, we then find relief by falling back on that for which we are gifted, our base ministry. If we never move into a phase ministry, however, there will be no growth.

THE HEXAGON

LEARNING TO PRAY ACCORDING TO THE MODEL
JESUS GAVE US IN THE LORD'S PRAYER
WILL RENEW YOUR CHURCH'S PRAYER LIFE.

CHAPTER 18

LIVING A LIFE OF PRAYER

One day Jesus was praying in a certain place. When he finished, one of his disciples said to him, "Lord, teach us to pray, just as John taught his disciples." ²He said to them, "When you pray, say: "'Father, hallowed be your name, your kingdom come. ³Give us each day our daily bread. ⁴Forgive us our sins, for we also forgive everyone who sins against us. And lead us not into temptation.'"

—Luke 11:1–4

The disciples—those whom Jesus called to be his full-time students—learned practical faith by watching Jesus in action. And, as we see throughout Scripture, Jesus spent much time in prayer. They recognized that Jesus' Up relationship with his Father through prayer was key to his fruitfulness in his ministry and relationships. Thus, when the disciples came to Jesus and say, "Lord, teach us to pray," we can assume they had been watching and listening to Jesus pray. There was something about the way their teacher went about prayer that was different and caused them to want to pray in the same way. ▲

In the classic book *With Christ in the School of Prayer*, author Andrew Murray notes, "Jesus never taught His disciples how to preach, only how to pray." Perhaps, having done life with Jesus, they understood better than we that prayer is what believers need most to be effective disciples of Christ. In

▲ FOR MORE ON UP, SEE THE TRIANGLE, CHAPTER 10.

fact, Andrew Murray issues this challenge to us: "What think you, my beloved fellow-disciples! Would it not be just what we need, to ask the Master for a month to give us a course of special lessons on the art of prayer?"[17]

Asking for a model of prayer was the next step in the disciples' spiritual growth. Jesus told them, "When you pray, pray like this." He did not give them several methods to choose from—he gave them one model to follow. It has only six parts to it, but it covers everything Jesus taught us about kingdom life:

Our Father in heaven, hallowed be your name,

Your kingdom come, your will be done on
earth as it is in heaven.

Give us today our daily bread.

Forgive us our debts, as we also have forgiven
our debtors.

And lead us not into temptation,

but deliver us from the evil one.

—Matthew 6:9–13

We as church leaders also have people watching us closely. Others learn from us and follow our example. What will they learn about prayer by watching us? Much, if we model the prayer Jesus taught. When we pray the six phrases of the Lord's Prayer, we are planting the seed of kingdom life in our hearts. This seed will sprout and grow, and the fruit will be meditative prayer, intercessory prayer, contemplative prayer, and so forth. The Hexagon invites us to go back to Jesus to learn how to pray.

God is most interested in relationship—an open, ongoing relationship that Scripture often describes as "walking with God." Life is a process of learning to walk with God, learning to relate and communicate with God. How we interact with God is vital for our lives. Thus, when Jesus is teaching his followers to pray, he is showing them how to walk with God. If walking with God truly is what our lives are all about, praying the way Jesus shows us is a major part of our life.

> Notice we said "model the prayer." When the disciples came to Jesus for help in prayer, he said, "When you pray, pray like this." He only taught one method of prayer. Now if we were the ones telling you, "This is how you should pray," you could say, "Well, I'll consider your thoughts, but I'm sure there are many other ways to do it." But when Jesus says, "Pray like this," we need to pay attention and do just as he says.
>
> —MIKE & WALT

The Lord's Prayer as taught by Jesus contains six elements. When we learn to pray these segments in the right way, we also will be learning to align our lives with God's will for us.

THE HEXAGON IN THE LORD'S PRAYER

Our Father in heaven. Jesus begins his prayer with a simple word that embodies an important relational concept: Father. Jesus uses the Aramaic word *Abba,* an informal name we often translate as *Daddy.* It's an intimate name for our intimate God. None of us will dispute that Jesus could legitimately start a conversation with the Almighty with such a familiar term. Yet how often do we fail to remember that in this prayer Jesus is teaching that all believers have the same right of relationship he enjoys? This relationship also transcends physical presence. God was just as much Jesus' Father during their physical separation—God in heaven and Jesus on earth—and he is just as much our Father now as he will be when we join him in heaven.

Hallowed be your name. God is very close and yet he is very different. We offer respect to our Father and our God for he is holy, with no darkness or sin. We pause to acknowledge that he is what we long to be. Our spirits yearn for this God-likeness to be a reality in us so that God's glory is revealed to others here on earth.

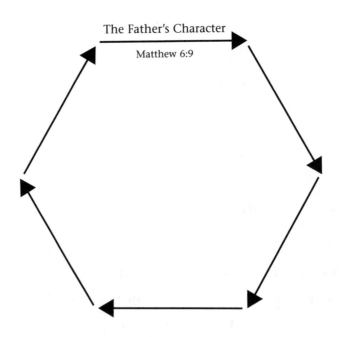

The Father's Character

Matthew 6:9

Your kingdom come, your will be done on earth as it is in heaven. Here Jesus says, "Yes, you've been fully adopted into God's family. You have every right to be talking to him but do you realize who your Daddy is? He's the King!" Not *a* king, *the* king. So we say, "I want what you want, Daddy. Your kingdom is an awesome kingdom of light and love, and I want your kingdom to advance in this world of darkness and hate. My desire is the same as your desire: to see everyone come out of this world of sin and into your kingdom of forgiveness. I want your rule to advance and be known in this world."

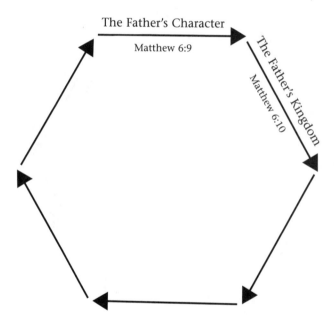

The Father's Character

Matthew 6:9

The Father's Kingdom

Matthew 6:10

Give us today our daily bread. As humans, we are needy beings. In prayer we can admit those needs. We have physical needs—food, shelter, clothing—that must be met daily. We need health in our bodies. We have spiritual and emotional needs—hope, someone to love, faith—that also must be cared for daily. We need strength in our spirits. All of this is included in "daily bread."

This is where we pull a chair up to our Father's table. We acknowledge that he has the means to feed us—whatever our hunger is. We go to him with our most basics needs anticipating he will feed us from his bounty. We ask because it demonstrates not only our need, but our trust in his provision for us.

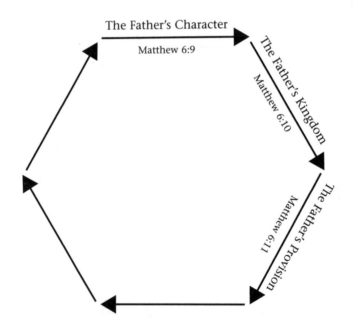

The Father's Character

Matthew 6:9

The Father's Kingdom

Matthew 6:10

Matthew 6:11

The Father's Provision

Forgive us our debts, as we also have forgiven our debtors. God has given us territory that is ours, and his provision within that territory is full and without want. Yet for some reason we often stray from our land and try to take what is not ours. We trespass into our neighbor's land and incur a debt we cannot pay. When we transgress against another we are saying, "God, what you have given to me is not enough." And for this we must ask forgiveness. We need to be aware that God has set a path for us; he has called us and given us a destiny. In this prayer we are asking God to help us not to stray from his place within his kingdom. And when other people stray from their path onto ours, hurting us and abusing us and causing us pain, then we need to forgive them as God has forgiven us. "Keep us, Lord, from being indebted to you in withholding forgiveness from others."

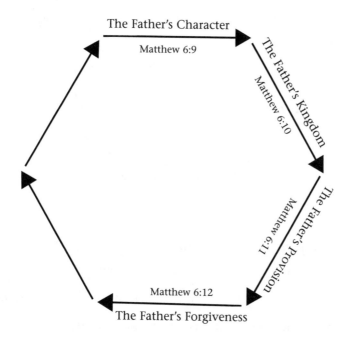

The Father's Character
Matthew 6:9
The Father's Kingdom
Matthew 6:10
The Father's Provision
Matthew 6:11
Matthew 6:12
The Father's Forgiveness

Lead us not into temptation. Up until now, the prayer has been dealing with our relationship with the Father and with those around us. Here the prayer changes, now dealing with us going out into the world with the message of God's love and forgiveness. "When you take us out into the world, Father, to do your bidding, to advance your kingdom, give us the strength to be in the world but not of the world."

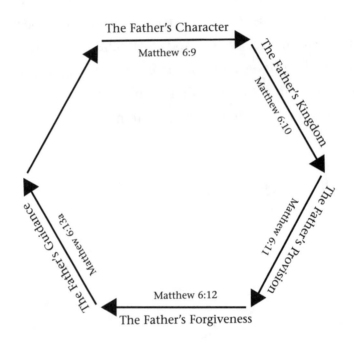

And deliver us from the evil one. Our souls have an enemy, and his devices of evil include temptation to participate in that evil. If we are led astray by his temptations, eventually we will end up in his hands. The evil one comes only to steal and to kill, says Jesus. He wants to steal our health, steal our joy and our love. If he is successful in his endeavors, we will enter into an eternal death in which we will forever be separated from the love of Christ. We are praying that God would keep us safe as we venture through life in the Lord's service.

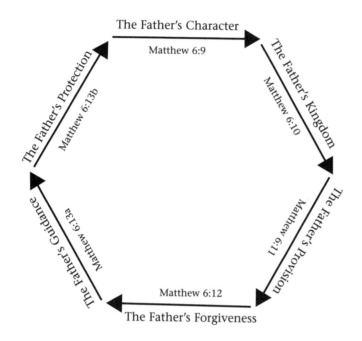

The Father's Character

Matthew 6:9

The Father's Protection

Matthew 6:13b

The Father's Kingdom

Matthew 6:10

The Father's Guidance

Matthew 6:13a

The Father's Provision

Matthew 6:11

Matthew 6:12

The Father's Forgiveness

As you study each section of the prayer you will to see that it is a framework in which to pour all of the thoughts and concerns of your life. The following chapter will help guide you with some practical steps on how to use this prayer for your own life and teach it practically to others. You'll also see how this model for prayer can add a new dimension to the prayer life of your church. You can take the thing most burning in your heart at the moment and pray through it using the prayer. Jesus teaches us as the model. In doing this, you are communicating with God as he has taught us to. It really is that simple.

YOU CAN TAKE THE THING MOST BURNING IN YOUR HEART AT THE MOMENT AND PRAY THROUGH IT USING THE PRAYER.

CHAPTER 19

PRACTICING THE SIX PRINCIPLES OF PRAYER

*B*y saying that there is only one prayer model given to us by Jesus, we do not mean to say that we pray these exact words and no more. When we say this model is simple, we do not mean that it is shallow. We must have a growing understanding of the six aspects of this prayer. We cannot remain static in our grasp of how Jesus taught us to pray—where there is no movement, there is no life. Too many churches have lifeless times of prayer, led by those who have remained in the shallow end of the pool. The model for prayer taught us by Jesus is shallow enough for a baby to bathe in and deep enough for elephants to swim through. What a marvelous paradox!

PRAYING THE HEXAGON

As you pray through this prayer, watch and wait— anticipate that God wants to speak to you through one of these areas. Picture the prayer as filling a bottle. You can apply it to your life in two ways. The first is to take your requests and drop them into the bottle. Pray through this model prayer with your request in mind, and see where it sticks. For instance, you can pray for your day:

> THE MODEL FOR PRAYER TAUGHT US BY JESUS IS SHALLOW ENOUGH FOR A BABY TO BATHE IN AND DEEP ENOUGH FOR ELEPHANTS TO SWIM THROUGH. WHAT A MARVELOUS PARADOX!

 FOR MORE ON GROWTH AND LIFE, SEE THE HEPTAGON, CHAPTERS 20 AND 21.

"Father, I know you are my caring, loving heavenly Father. You rule over all and will watch over me today from your throne in heaven. Let your glory be seen in all I do today. I want your rule and will to be done in all of my thoughts and actions today. Please provide for all of my needs today—spiritual, physical, financial."

Here is where it sticks: you begin to think about the drawer full of bills you need to pay, but you are not sure where the money is going to come from. You spend your time in prayer seeking God for the "daily bread" to pay your debts. This is the point in praying through the Lord's Prayer that you stop; you realize that it is the area of your life that you and God need to walk through together today. Tomorrow the stopping point might be for forgiveness or for help in times of temptation. Each day will have at least one place that sticks out and grabs you as you pour your prayer from the bottle.

The second way to use this model prayer is to pour it out over each request. If someone you know is sick and asks you to pray for them, you can pray like this:

"Father, your reign in heaven extends down to our residence here on earth. Let your glory be seen in the life of my friend. In your kingdom there is no sickness, no pain. Let your kingdom come in my friend's life and body today. Providing our daily bread and our daily provisions includes having a healthy body so we can do all of your will, so please give my friend a healthy body today. Forgive my friend, as he forgives others, knowing that unforgiveness in our spirits can cause our bodies to react as well. Let him not be tempted to turn from you, his Healer, in this time of need. And protect him from the principalities and powers that want to cause him harm."

As you continue practicing the prayer, it becomes much easier to invite the Holy Spirit to prompt you to "stick" on one area at a time, whether you are praying for yourself or someone else. For instance, as you pray through the Lord's Prayer, perhaps you will think, "I am really having a problem with so-and-so in my small group. He has stomped in my garden over and over again. He is out of his territory and into mine. Nevertheless, I forgive him, Lord, just as you forgive me when I stomp in someone else's garden." Perhaps you will stop on *"your kingdom come, your will be done"* as you consider what is going on in our world. You may be thinking of an atrocity done to people in another country. You say, "Lord, this does not look like your kingdom. Hate, not love, is reigning there, and that is not right. Let your kingdom rule be seen right now in that situation, and let love—which I know is your will—be felt by those people."

> AS YOU CONTINUE PRACTICING THE PRAYER, IT BECOMES MUCH EASIER TO INVITE THE HOLY SPIRIT TO PROMPT YOU TO "STICK" ON ONE AREA AT A TIME.

There are several more ways we find it helpful to use the Lord's Prayer to deepen our communication with the Father. As you reflect on these methods, no doubt you will come up with more on your own.

HOW DEEP DOES THE HEXAGON GO?

Take one phrase per day from the Lord's Prayer and focus on it for your prayer time. Spend one day just thinking about what calling the God of the universe *Father* really means. If he truly is your Father, what responsibilities does he have toward you? What do you have in your relationship with him? What does it mean that he is in heaven? Reflect on Dallas Willard's words: "Heaven is God breaking into our reality."

EACH DAY, PRAY THROUGH ONE OF THE PHRASES. USE THAT PHRASE TO PRAY FOR THE NEEDS IN YOUR LIFE AND IN THE LIVES OF THOSE AROUND YOU.

Each day, pray through one of the phrases. Use that phrase to pray for the needs in your life and in the lives of those around you. If you feel you have reached the bottom of that phrase, that there is no more for you to get out of it, dig some more. Each of the six segments of this prayer is bottomless.

Another way to better understand the Lord's Prayer is to see it as a circular prayer; each phrase is fully developed by all of the others. Take one phrase, place a colon after it, and then continue with the other phrases. Ask, how is this part of the prayer fully articulated in the rest of the prayer. For instance, take *"your kingdom come, your will be done"*:

"Give us today our daily bread." It is God's loving desire to meet all of our needs. In his kingdom, there is no want

"Forgive us our debts." In God's kingdom, our sins are washed away, never to be revisited.

"As we also have forgiven our debtors." As we walk in the grace of God's forgiveness, we will forgive others. Freely we have received, freely we give. This is a law of kingdom life.

"Lead us not into temptation." It is God's will that we walk the path he has laid out for us. In his kingdom, we will be fulfilled by all he has for us, and will not turn aside for a lesser, temporary fix.

"Deliver us from the evil one." The kingdom of God is all light; in it, darkness disappears. Principalities and powers that haunt us have no power in God's kingdom.

"Our Father in heaven." The kingdom is ruled by a king—and the king is our dad! We can feel right at home in the kingdom. We are not strangers, but sons and daughters. We belong in God's kingdom.

You can do this with any of the phrases in the Lord's Prayer. Put a colon on the end, and keep reading the rest of the phrases. Consider how that segment is played out in your life in the light of the rest of the prayer.

Let us suggest one final way to dig deeper into Jesus' model for prayer. We've mentioned praying until the Holy Spirit stops you. Using this method, focus on where you are stopped, and use your "sticking point" as a starting point. Ask yourself, "To what extent have I chosen to act like God in this area?" If you focus on "daily bread," think about how you are taking God's place and are striving to meet your own needs. Then look left and right, as it were, at the other phrases. How are you supplanting God in these areas? This can lead to a time of repentance, cleansing us from the toxins that build up in us when we assume God's role.

These are just a few ways to explore these six short phrases Jesus gave us as a model for our prayers. As you can see, there is no end to how we can walk and talk with God using this model. As you begin using the principles of the Hexagon in your personal prayer life, you will no doubt uncover many other ways to apply this model. We encourage you also to begin teaching these principles to your staff and church family. We believe you will see exciting changes in the prayer life of your church.

THE HEPTAGON

GOD'S PEOPLE ARE A LIVING ORGANISM
SUBJECT TO THE SAME PRINCIPLES OF GROWTH
THAT APPLY TO ALL LIVING THINGS.
MRS GREN CAN HELP YOU
GROW A HEALTHY CHURCH.

CHAPTER 20

PRACTICING THE PRINCIPLES
OF A VITAL LIFE

As you come to him, the living Stone—rejected by men but chosen by God and precious to him— ⁵*you also, like living stones, are being built into a spiritual house to be a holy priesthood, offering spiritual sacrifices acceptable to God through Jesus Christ.*

—1 Peter 2:4–5

*C*hurch health and growth is all about life—the body of Christ being an organism rather than an organization. And life gets messy sometimes, doesn't it? So it's easier for us to deal with organizations because we can control organizations. Think of it this way: organisms are to organizations what the horse is to the cart. Many churches "put the cart before the horse," building facilities and programs before they have adequately taken care of the needs of the people. It's not the cart that will get things moving—it's the horse that provides the power to move the cart. We need to feed and care for the horse, but instead our energy goes into the cart, so the horse ends up too weak to pull the cart.

There are other analogies that can be drawn from this metaphor. Like organizations, carts have interchangeable parts—if a wheel breaks, you can replace it. The parts of an organism are inextricably interdependent. Even a healthy horse will weaken and die if it is not properly cared for and nourished. Granted, a cart is much easier to take care of. We can paint it, decorate it any way we want, show it off to our friends. Horses sometimes wander off on their own and don't always respond like we want. So that's why so many leaders in the church choose to build carts and ignore the horses. Maybe the question we need to ask ourselves is, what good is a cart when the horse is dead!

KEEPING THE HORSE ALIVE

A lot of our "horses" at Joy left when they saw a new cart coming down the road. We used to talk about all of our great programs and plan big building projects. But people aren't interested in that anymore. I had to realize that I had been working hard building an organization when God is interested in organism, in life. That is what the Heptagon, MRS GREN, is about.

—WALT

People will come where they see evidence of life. As Helen Keller said, "Life is an adventure or it is nothing." A church that resources programs and property at the expense of the life of the people is nothing. If you still think that "If you build it, they will come," you are deceiving yourself. The future church must be a living organism not an organization. Every church is just one generation away from extinction, and today's generation wants to see living stones. Life in the Spirit is the grandest adventure of all. Once we start modeling life in the Spirit, the people will come.

EVERY CHURCH IS JUST ONE GENERATION AWAY FROM EXTINCTION.

ORGANIC LIVING

We are told in Scripture that we have life in the Spirit, but what does that really mean? Jesus gives us pictures of this life through many of his stories and teachings that deal with biological life. Life in the Spirit resembles organic life, just on a different plane.

Jesus started off his ministry by clearly declaring what he came to do. He was here to plant the kingdom of God into our hearts, to inaugurate the rule of God in our lives. And to show us what the kingdom life looks like, Jesus used stories involving snapshots from ordinary life: agriculture, parents and children, the relationship between friends, money matters, coins that are lost, sheep that are found.

When you track these stories through Scripture you find that Jesus often relies on the subject of biological life. The kingdom of God is a seed, it is the sowing of seeds on various soils, it is a vineyard. Take this beyond the Gospels to the rest of the New Testament. What is the community of believers called? The body of Christ. God often uses biological life as a metaphor for what he wants our churches to look like.

MEET MRS GREN

Biology—the study of life and all living organisms. In school you learned (or should have learned) about the seven characteristics of life that identify all living organisms. These seven signposts of life are

Movement	**G**rowth
Respiration	**R**eproduction
Sensitivity	**E**xcretion
	Nutrition

THESE SEVEN PROCESSES CAN BE A USEFUL DIAGNOSTIC FOR ASSESSING THE HEALTH OF YOUR CHURCH.

Children in Great Britain commit these seven processes to memory using the acronym MRS GREN. And that is what we call our seven-sided shape (the Heptagon) in LifeShapes: MRS GREN, or life in the kingdom of God. These seven processes can be a useful diagnostic for assessing the health of your church.

MOVEMENT: SHOW YOU'RE NOT DEAD

Movement is an indication of life and usually occurs in response to stimuli. Consider animals in the wild. They prefer to lie in the cool shade of a tree or in a den dug into the ground. But when threatened by a predator, they move—quickly. And when they are hungry or thirsty, they must move to hunt or they will die. Animals move when stimulated by an outer (danger) or inner (hunger) force. Plants exhibit movement through growth, so the effect is sometimes so slow it is hard to detect.

The Old Testament is a series of stories about patriarchs, prophets, and people on the move. We see this principle at work in Exodus 14: the children of Israel have left Egypt, but hesitate at the crossing of the Red Sea. Behind them lies a life of slavery to Pharaoh, but before them they see only a very, scary unknown. They stop moving. How much easier it seems to stand still in what we know, regardless of how unfulfilling, than to move into the unknown!

You would think that seeing Pharaoh's army rushing after them would be sufficient stimuli to get them moving again, but they allow fear to paralyze them. Their leader tells them to stand firm, but God says, "Move on!" It is not until they get moving again that they see the miraculous power of God in their midst.

The alive church is the church on the move. God uses many different methods to stimulate movement—his Word, his Spirit, persecution—because his desire is to see the living church reaching out to our dying world. What about your church? Are you moving? Don't be afraid to move on, even if you don't know yet where you will end up.

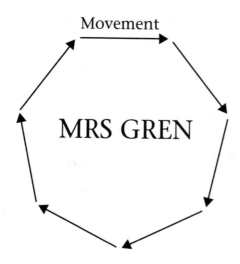

Movement

MRS GREN

RESPIRATION: BREATHING GOD'S BREATH

Respiration is not synonymous with breathing. Every cell in your body has a powerhouse called the mitochondrion that releases energy. This is respiration. The powerhouse is dependent on oxygen that is brought into the body through breathing. So breathing is absolutely necessary for respiration, and the respiration process is essential for energy to be released for the body to function. A living organism cannot "make" energy, it can only release it.

Breathing may be natural for most living organisms, but for many

> One of the painful realities of dealing with living organisms is acknowledging that things die. Like doctors in a hospital trauma room, we as church leaders have a responsibility to monitor the vital signs of efforts within our churches and be willing to "call it" when there is no hope. Sometimes a little spiritual CPR—a fresh breath from God—is all that is needed to bring vitality back. However, both of us have had to let things die when they have failed to thrive and have then watched as God raised up something new.
>
> —MIKE & WALT

humans in the Western world, breathing correctly is a dying art (no pun intended). Several studies indicate that our ability to breathe effectively has significantly diminished over the last few decades, resulting in loss of vitality and quality of life. In general, we are bad breathers and it's killing us.[18]

Bad breathing can be the result of many factors: illness, lack of exercise, fear, pollution. Sometimes it's just us holding our breath—like a child throwing a temper tantrum—in a vain attempt to exert control. In the same way, many of us are bad spiritual breathers. Just as our breathing oxygen releases energy in our bodies, God's breathing into us releases the energy of his Spirit in our lives. When we breathe deeply of the breath of God, we discover that the energy of God to complete the task at hand is released within us.

As ministers to the body of Christ, we need to encourage our people to breathe deeply again. Ole Hallesby says that prayer is to the soul what breathing is to the body. Prayer is the breath of God filling us up again. What might be making your church breathless, robbing you of vitality? How can you encourage others to practice a life of prayer—inhaling God's Spirit and exhaling his will? God wants the very power of heaven to be loosed in our lives, and it comes by spiritual respiration.

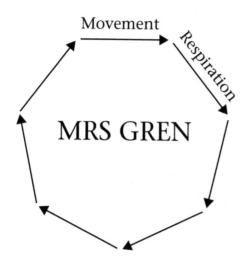

SENSITIVITY: THE PENTAGON AT WORK

Your body is not a bunch of independent parts randomly stuck together. It all works as one unit. The first function we looked at was movement. We said that living organisms move according to stimuli. Sensitivity is what enables the body to sense the stimulation and know that it must move. Thus, sensitivity plays a vital role in life.

Sensitivity is important in the church. The body of Christ has various senses just as the human body does. There is sensitivity to sight, to hearing, to touch, to smell, and to taste (or, in this case, speech) that must be active in the church for it to be living. We see this active in the church through the fivefold gifts Paul mentions in Ephesians 4—what we refer to as the Pentagon.

A healthy, living church needs Christians who are sensitive to the needs and pains of others, believers who can laugh with those who laugh and cry with those who cry. This is the sensitivity of touch and is found in believers whose base ministry is pastor. We also need those who are sensitive to sight, in this case foresight given by God. These are the prophets.

The church needs people who will be sensitive to hearing others, listening actively, and then instructing them on how to proceed. These are our teachers. Those sensitive in speech, being gifted to share the Good News on any occasion, are the evangelists. And those who can sniff out staleness and know it is time to move forward are the apostles, sensitive to the move of God to explore new territory for the kingdom. God wants us all to be sensitive to his stimuli so that we will move and act as he directs.

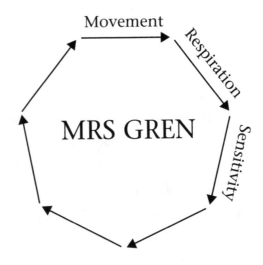

GROWTH: THE INEVITABLE RESULT OF A HEALTHY LIFE

Growth is a natural process of living things. It is an expression of life. Are you growing? Sometimes it is hard to tell. We don't see growth every day. It

FOR MORE ON THIS PRINCIPLE, SEE THE PENTAGON, CHAPTER 16.

comes through the natural rhythms of life. But growth must always be occurring in a living being. When you stop growing, you die. It's that simple.

What about your church? Is your church growing? The same thing applies to the church—stop growing and the church will die. Let's break it down a bit more. Are the small groups in your church growing? Are the individuals who make up the church growing in their faith? As a church leader, you must constantly be aware of what is growing and what is showing signs of no growth and thus decay and death. As we see in the Semi-Circle, growth takes place as we swing in the rhythm between abiding and fruitfulness. ◗

We are not told to work for our growth. God is the one who causes us to grow. (Look at 1 Cor. 3:6–9 and Col. 2:19.) But there are things we can do to create a growing environment, both individually and corporately. As a matter of fact, if the other six aspects of MRS GREN are operating properly, growth will occur spontaneously. So let us move on to reproduction.

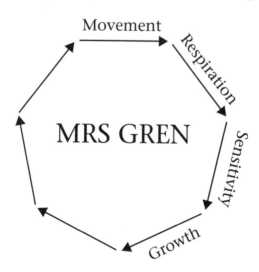

Movement

Respiration

MRS GREN

Sensitivity

Growth

FOR MORE ON ABIDING AND FRUITFULNESS, SEE THE SEMI-CIRCLE, CHAPTER 7.

CHAPTER 21

SIGNS OF LIFE

Today's church is giving birth to the church of tomorrow. Many churches are in the transitional phase of birthing—often the most painful and discouraging phase. It is important during this time of transition to monitor closely the vital signs of the church. The seven signs of life represented by the Heptagon, affectionately called MRS GREN, can help you do just that. Let's continue to look at how the principles of MRS GREN can be applied to church life.

REPRODUCTION . . . CREATING THE FUTURE

Reproduction is different from growth in that it is a multiplication of the organism. All living things reproduce by bringing together two disparate elements and then fusing them together into a new element. A sperm and an egg, living cells unto themselves, come together to form a new organism, in appearance like that of the "donors" of the sperm and egg. Reproduction has taken place.

In our spiritual life, God takes our words (sharing the Good News of God's forgiveness in the person of Jesus) and fuses them with the heart of one open to this Good News to make a new spirit—one that is alive, born from above. This is reproduction on the spiritual level. One Christian has become two. From these two will come four. A small group will form, and soon it will be multiplied into more small groups, forming a church. Reproduction is a sign of life.

FOR THE CHURCH, CREATING A HEALTHY NEXT GENERATION IS THE MOST IMPORTANT TARGET WE HAVE.

There seems to be a mechanism within the created order that prevents unhealthy specimens from being multiplied. The unhealthy ones generally don't multiply; it is the healthy that carry on the species. It is the goal of a species to create a healthy next generation, the most important target of their lives. For the church, creating a healthy next generation is the most important target we have.

Look at Europe. Children, teenagers, and young adults don't attend church any longer. Why is that? It is because Christians in Europe have forsaken the reproduction of themselves into a new generation. There really is not a "next generation" of Christians in Europe. Perhaps it is because the older generations of Christians were not healthy. God will do a new thing—spark new growth—in Europe, but it is not going to come in the natural order of things. Our primary cry must be for the children to come. We must say with the psalmist, "Don't let me die, Lord, until I speak of your

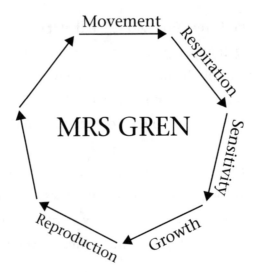

power to the next generation" (Psalm 71 paraphrase). How are you doing in bringing forth children for the kingdom? Is reproduction important to you? It should be—it is a signal that you and your church are alive.

EXCRETION: A CLEANSED LIFE

"Okay," you say, "I can see how the other six biological processes can be applied to the church. But not excretion. That's just gross!" Well, you would be wrong. We see this natural part of life in the proclamation Jesus made at the beginning of his ministry: "Repent and believe the good news."

Every heart builds up a collection of junk throughout the day that needs to be emptied through the process of repentance. If we do not get rid of these sins, they will act just like toxin does in the human body, causing illness and, eventually, death. Jesus made it clear: Forgive others so God can forgive you. Research is now showing that unforgiveness causes increased blood pressure, hormonal changes, cardiovascular disease, and impaired brain functions, including memory loss. Not excreting what others have done to us is just as unhealthy as not getting rid of our own sins.

If you don't excrete in your natural life, aside from looking really nasty and feeling very uncomfortable, you will die. That's just a medical fact. Toxins build up within you and cause vital organs to stop working. Eventually your entire body shuts down—permanently. The writer of Hebrews calls these toxins building up within us "the root of bitterness." We are told to remove it—rip it out.

For the body of Christ, excretion comes in the form of repentance and discipline. Oswald Chambers says that "The entrance into the Kingdom is through

> FOR THE BODY OF CHRIST, EXCRETION COMES IN THE FORM OF REPENTANCE AND DISCIPLINE.

the panging pains of repentance crashing into a man's respectable good-ness;" and that it is the Holy Spirit "Who produces these agonies."[19]

In some cases, church discipline requires that an unrepentant brother be expelled, as Paul instructs the church at Corinth, in order to give him the opportunity to come back to the life of faith. Whether in our individual lives or in the lives of our churches, we must not embrace wickedness, and we cannot accommodate sin in any form. It must be excreted for us to remain healthy.

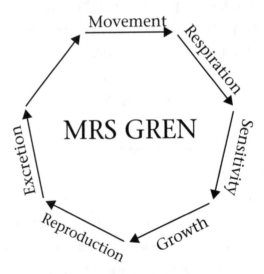

NUTRITION: THE OBEDIENCE DIET

Finally, we have nutrition. All living things must take in nutrients or they will die. In this era of carb-free this and fat-free that, we have an even greater awareness of what proper nutrition is. For the spiritual diet, there is but one main course.

"I am the bread of life," declares Jesus. To live, we must dine on his words, his actions, his commands. We can break this down even further. When Jesus met with the woman at the well (John 4), his disciples had gone off to a nearby village to buy food. When they came back, they offered some to Jesus.

"I have food to eat that you don't know about," he said. The disciples wondered just where he got this food and what it was. Perhaps they were jealous, thinking it was probably better than what they had to eat. Then Jesus spelled it out clearly for them.

> WHEN WE OBEY THE COMMANDS OF JESUS, OUR SOULS ARE FED.

"My food is doing the will of my father," he told them. Obeying God is our nutrition. When we obey the commands of Jesus, our souls are fed. We feel full and fulfilled.

Without nutrition, you will die. There is no way around that. Without the right kind of nutrition, you will die slowly. In the same way, our churches will die if there is not a regular feeding on Jesus, the very Word of God. We must clearly and consistently proclaim his teachings. But we can't stop there. We must obey his commands to get our fill of nutrition vital for our growth.

There she is—MRS GREN.

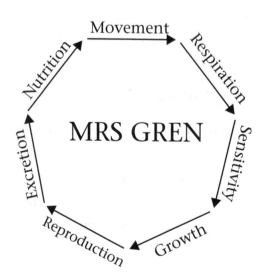

A HEALTHY SELF-EXAMINATION

> WE MUST MAKE A CONSCIOUS EFFORT TO COMPARE OUR LIVES WITH THE HEALTHY LIFE DESCRIBED BY JESUS.

So now the question is, what do we do with MRS GREN? Knowing that Jesus often used biological illustrations in his storytelling does not mean we will automatically apply the teachings to our lives. We must make a conscious effort to compare our lives with the healthy life described by Jesus.

Doctors say that most cancers can be completely cured if they are found in time. Thus, we are taught how to check our bodies for potential signs of cancer or other disease so we can catch it, cure it, and continue living. Just as we conduct self-examinations on our physical bodies, we need to perform self-exams spiritually. The seven processes MRS GREN teaches us makes a thorough exam possible. Go through each of the seven processes of life in this way, checking your own pulse as it were. When you find an area you have been neglecting, give it more attention. Don't wait until disease sets in and you need emergency-room care. Teach these principles for a vital life to those you lead in your church. If every follower of Jesus were to maintain all seven functions of life in their spiritual life, there would be no need for pastors to be counselors. Imagine that!

GROWTH CYCLE OF CHURCH GROUPS

God has designed us to live as social creatures, so it would be difficult for us to be living beings in any genuine sense without authentic community. It would appear from a study of the Scriptures that we can draw certain conclusions about groups, their sizes and functions, and how we as leaders should build community. Scripture is also instructive on how the proper use of groups can alleviate the overwhelming burden of ministry so many pastors are experiencing.

> [17]*Moses' father-in-law replied, "What you are doing is not good.* [18]*You and these people who come to you will only wear yourselves out. The work is too heavy for you; you cannot handle it alone."*

—Exodus 18:17–18

Ever feel like Moses in this passage? Trying to lead a consumer-driven, staff-driven, program-driven church organization is a sure prescription for burnout. Like all good father figures, Jethro tells his son-in-law Moses, "Hey, man! You can't do it all and you can't do it alone. For your sake and the sake of your people, you need to try something different. God's got a better plan."

Yes, God has a plan for the healthy distribution of leadership among groups and it looks something like this:

Nation
Tribe
Thousands
Hundreds
Fifties
Tens
Twos and threes

Jethro advised Moses to establish leaders of thousands, hundreds, fifties, and tens along with the leaders of the twelve tribes. Above the twelve tribes was the nation of Israel itself led by Moses under God's authority. Following Jethro's advice, Moses identified qualified and equipped men (vs. 21) over these various size groups. The tens may have represented the average expected size of the nuclear family at that time and for that culture, but in today's society the smallest group would be a couple formed by marriage.

From any reading of the books of Moses, we can see that the national and tribal leaders of Israel were already in place, and marriages were happening all the time. What Moses had failed to recognize was that there was a need for a more complete infrastructure of leaders and groups in order for the people of God to be in effective relationship with God himself, with each other, and with the world at large.

> ONE OF THE KINGDOM TASKS ASSIGNED TO GOD'S PEOPLE IS TO REBUILD HUMAN COMMUNITY WHEREVER WE CAN.

Interestingly, Jesus seemed to follow a similar pattern: he sent out disciples in pairs (obviously not *married* pairs). He called together a team of twelve out of a team of seventy-two. Then on the day of Pentecost, there were about 120 waiting as Jesus had instructed for the promised Holy Spirit, after which the church had thousands in its community. These may have been organized naturally along ethnic lines. This would provide one explanation for why the apostles had to intervene to make sure that the least prominent group within the church had a fair share of the church's resources (Acts 6).

It is not our intention to argue for an overly tight application of these insights into the development of Christian community, but to offer a reflective tool as we seek to develop living communities within our shifting western culture. One of the kingdom tasks assigned to God's people is to rebuild human community wherever we can. Again, our experience leads us to conclude that this will involve the emergence of a spectrum of groups in different shapes and sizes. If we are to be strategic as leaders, we need to know where to begin. Many sociologists and anthropologists think that the most important component of human society is the extended family.

Our experience confirms that churches should focus on the development of "clusters," the extended family-size group of between twenty and seventy. To do this we will need to raise up from among our people leaders who carry this vision and are capable of overseeing these groups and the long-range task of rebuilding our communities and culture. Watch for additional resources from LifeShapes on this important subject.

Life in community is what the church is all about. Looking at your ministry in the light of MRS GREN helps identify trouble spots before they become full-fledged illness and incurable disease. Without really getting caught up in the contemporary debate about the role and ministry of the Holy Spirit, we have begun to describe his work as the bringer of life. As we maintain openness to him, we will exhibit more of the life that he brings.

THE OCTAGON

EVANGELISM WILL TAKE ON A NEW PERSPECTIVE
AS YOU LEARN TO DISCOVER THE PERSON OF PEACE
AND HOW THE PROCESS WORKS FROM GOD'S PERSPECTIVE.

CHAPTER 22

LIVING A MISSION-MINDED LIFE

After this the Lord appointed seventy-two others and sent them two by two ahead of him to every town and place where he was about to go. 2He told them, "The harvest is plentiful, but the workers are few. Ask the Lord of the harvest, therefore, to send out workers into his harvest field. 3Go! I am sending you out like lambs among wolves. 4Do not take a purse or bag or sandals; and do not greet anyone on the road. 5"When you enter a house, first say, 'Peace to this house.' 6If a man of peace is there, your peace will rest on him; if not, it will return to you.

—Luke 10:1–6

The destiny of the church is directly tied to how passionate she remains to her mission. In past decades, our zeal to fulfill the Great Commission has often led to the great omission—we've made converts without making disciples fully trained and equipped in all Jesus taught. As the Church, we are all to participate in God's command to go and make disciples according to the model that Jesus has given us.

How we approach outreach in today's culture has fallen under scrutiny in recent years, and rightly so. Many of the techniques that have worked in the past are obviously not working as well anymore. We need to return yet again to the Compass—Jesus.

We've already stated that Jesus was the wisest man that ever lived, as well as the best leader and teacher. It just makes sense that he would also be the best at evangelism. In his book *Permission Evangelism*, Michael Simpson looks at Jesus' interaction with the rich, young ruler (Mark 10) and sums it up this way:

"Christ was evangelizing, but it sure doesn't look like the way most people do it today. Even though it says Jesus loved him, he stood there and let the man walk away. Why did Christ not follow him when he walked away? Why didn't he try harder when this man seemed so eager? Why didn't Jesus 'get him saved' before addressing this difficult area of his life [his riches]?

Christ didn't run after the rich young ruler because he knew the young man's heart wasn't ready. Jesus knew and let him walk. Jesus never ran after anyone. Instead, he made himself available to those willing to wholeheartedly seek the Way to God, the Truth about God, and the Life found in God."[20]

Our eighth shape, the Octagon, is about sharing the Good News in the same way that Jesus did and as he taught his disciples to do. Don't let the fact that our Octagon has eight sides put you off. We are not going to load you down with eight major theological lessons or eight principles you need to memorize. The Octagon has one key message: find the Person of Peace.

PERSON OF PEACE

As Jesus commissioned the seventy-two disciples to go ahead of him, proclaiming the coming of the kingdom of God, he gave them directions for how to proceed.

"When you enter a house, first say, 'Peace to this house.' If a man of peace is there, your peace will rest on him; if not, it will return to you" (Luke 10: 5–6).

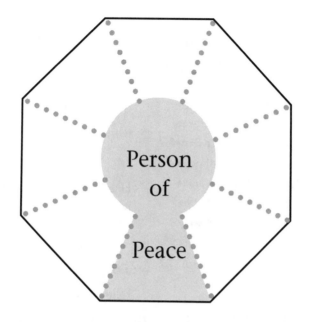

Jesus' message to his disciples then, and to us today, is that as we are walking in this world, we are to be on the lookout for a Person of Peace. Who is this Person of Peace, and how do we recognize him?

Very simply, a Person of Peace is one who is prepared to hear the message of the kingdom and the King. He is ready to receive what God will give you to say at that moment. This should be our prayer as we venture forth each day. "Lord, bring into my path today a Person of Peace, and give me the grace to speak your words to this person." One who is not a Person of Peace will not receive what you have to say. We are not to belabor the issue. Jesus says to shake the dust off your feet and move on. No amount of coercion on our part can make someone become a Person of Peace. This is the job of the Holy Spirit; he alone can prepare a heart to hear the Gospel. Our job

A PERSON OF PEACE IS ONE WHO IS PREPARED TO HEAR THE MESSAGE OF THE KINGDOM AND THE KING.

Finding the Person of Peace is Jesus' strategy for kingdom expansion. It is not just for what we think of as witnessing. It is seeing an opening and walking through it. Walt is my Person of Peace. God has, through him, opened a door for me to share LifeShapes with others. He is the one God brought to me to make this happen. I am so thankful that he was willing to listen to God and obey him.

—MIKE

is to have our spiritual eyes open, looking for a Person of Peace to cross our paths. Perhaps this concept will make more sense as we see it modeled by Paul when he went out on his missions trips.

HOW PAUL FOUND THE PERSON OF PEACE

We read in Acts 16 that Paul, along with Silas, Timothy, and Luke, made plans where to go next, but were "kept by the Holy Spirit from preaching the word in the province of Asia." They then turned toward Bithynia, but once again the Spirit kept them from going there. Then in the night Paul had a vision of a man in Macedonia crying out for help. Right away they packed up and set out for Macedonia.

Once they arrived in the Macedonian city of Philippi, Paul set forth to find a Person of Peace, someone prepared to receive the Word of God. It was the Sabbath, and Paul knew he would find devout Jews and "God-fearers" (Gentiles who worshipped God and adhered to the Jewish scriptures) by the river praying as the custom was. When they found a group of women there, Paul—a rabbi by training—assumed the role of a teacher and sat down.

As he proclaimed the Gospel, the Lord opened the heart of one woman, a dealer in purple cloth named Lydia. Paul recognized that she was a Person of Peace for that moment. We don't know what he said to her, or her exact words in response. We do know that she and her household were all baptized into the faith, and Paul and his friends stayed with Lydia while they continued to plant a church in Philippi.

They stayed in Philippi long enough that they became regulars at the riverside prayer meetings. One time as they were heading for the river, a slave girl possessed by a demon spirit followed them shouting, "These men are servants of the Most High God, who are telling you the way to be saved." Surely this must be a Person of Peace! This was an open door for evangelism if ever there was one, right?

Paul did not see it that way. He commanded the evil spirit to leave the girl, which it did immediately. The problem was the girl, under the influence of the evil spirit, could tell the future and was being used by her masters to make large amounts of money. Now her masters were furious that their way to wealth had been torn out from underneath them. They dragged Paul and Silas before the magistrates, and the apostles were beaten and thrown in prison.

Once again, even in the confines of these circumstances, Paul was on the lookout for a Person of Peace. This time, it came in the form of the jailor who guarded them. You are familiar with the story: around midnight, as Paul and Silas were

When we first arrived at our home in Brixton, our garden was riddled with broken glass. I spent many hours picking this out to make our yard safe for our young children. This tedious task was not aided by the constant presence our young teenage neighbor, Carl. I felt Carl was a pain in the neck, his chats consuming too much of my time. My wife, Sally, saw him differently. She sensed that he was a Person of Peace— someone who could make a significant difference in the neighborhood. Sally's insight changed my perspective on Carl and Sally proved to be right. Carl soon became a Christian, along with his Mum, Dad, and his sister who is now a missionary in India.

—*MIKE*

singing worship songs, an earthquake shook the prison so that all the chains were loosed and all the doors flung open. The jailor thought the prisoners must have escaped and, saving his commanding officer the trouble, set about to take his own life.

"Don't harm yourself!" shouted Paul. "We are all here!"

"Sirs, what must I do to be saved?" cried the jailor.

As Paul was present in the jail (not by his choice, but there he was), the person God had prepared presented himself, and Paul walked through the open door.

> IT IS NO GOOD TRYING TO FORCE OPEN DOORS THAT GOD HAS NOT OPENED, AND WE MUST NOT BE DISTRACTED SO THAT WE MISS THE DOORS HE HAS OPENED.

The Person of Peace is someone God has prepared for that specific time. It is no good trying to force open doors that God has not opened, and we must not be distracted so that we miss the doors he has opened. This really is exciting news. Even in the most important task we have been given, the assignment to go and make disciples, God does most of the work. Our main job is to walk through life with our eyes open and our ears listening to the Spirit as he reveals to us the Person of Peace he has prepared.

CHAPTER 23

EMPOWERING EVANGELISM

*O*ur outward relationships are not just to be occasional outreach projects or evangelism programs. We are to live a lifestyle of mission, evangelism, and service. Jesus explained his mission imperative to his disciples as "the reason I have come" (Mark 1:38). He spoke of sending his followers as the Father had sent him (John 20:21), commissioned them as disciple-makers (Matt. 28:19), and described them as his witnesses in continually-expanding spheres until their message reached the ends of the earth (Acts 1:8). In every account of Jesus addressing his disciples (the twelve and the seventy-two), he recounted their mission. This biblical strategy for evangelism is the focus of the Octagon.

PERCEIVING THE PERSON OF PEACE

There are seven other principles in our model but the Person of Peace is the key so let's take a look at five things to keep in mind as you look for the Person of Peace before we move on.

Time

Jesus preceded his sending the disciples with an exhortation that there are specific times and places the harvest is ripe (John 4:34–38). He links this discernment with an observation: lift up your eyes. Not every section of society, sub-culture, or individual is equally ready and open to the Gospel. In some contexts we need to sow, while in others we should be prepared to reap. Part of our mission task is to have God's perspective showing us where there is a spiritual openness. Remember what we learned with the Triangle: before we can have an outward relationship, we must have the upward connection. ▲

> AS KINGDOM WORKERS, OUR JOB IS TO LEARN TO DISCERN THE SEASON OF EACH PERSON'S SOUL.

Every church is to be involved in both sowing and reaping. Many of our current ways of doing church might make us uncomfortable with what Jesus is telling us here. Jesus says we should be glad to invest in a harvest even though the benefit of our labor might go to the church down the street. If our mission is the expansion of the kingdom, it shouldn't matter who reaps the benefit of our labor. As kingdom workers, our job is to learn to discern the season of each person's soul. Is it sowing time or reaping time?

Team

Our inward relationships lead to our outward ministry. We are not called to go it alone, as we have seen in our dicussions of the inward dimension of the Triangle and in our discussion of the contrast between organizations and living organism (MRS GREN). The mission-minded church will develop a team model for evangelism.

There are good reasons for this even apart from the fact that it is the way Jesus did it. In our culture today, longing to belong makes authentic community a very powerful drawing force. Just as in the times of the early church, unbelievers are compelled to check out the message of such groups. This principle can be seen in the ministry of Paul. He is constantly referring

▲ FOR MORE ON UP AND IN, SEE THE TRIANGLE, CHAPTERS 10 AND 11.

to his teammates—Barnabas, Silas, Timothy, Titus. Jesus' presence is promised wherever two or three believers are together (Matt. 18:20).

Target

Jesus was very strategic in his outreach. He knew he could not be everywhere at once, and neither could his disciples. He focused their outreach on the lost sheep of the house of Israel (Matt. 10:6) and warned them against being distracted by those not ready to receive their message (Luke 9:5 and 10:4). In mission and evangelism we should look for people who are open to us and our message. We should concentrate on these receptive people of peace, and not force dialogue or relationship where it does not naturally flow.

Task

The assignment for the disciple is to share the Good News of the kingdom with the Person of Peace, whenever and wherever that person is found. How do we recognize the Person of Peace? According to the instructions Jesus gave his disciples in Matthew 10 and Luke 10, the Person of Peace will:

- Welcome you. If he does not, you are to "shake the dust off your feet" as you leave his home. (Matt. 10:14)
- Listen to you. Those who listen to you are listening to Jesus. (Luke 10:16)
- Serve or support you. We must allow a Person of Peace to serve us. (Matt. 10:10)

Many in our churches feel very uncomfortable when they hear the word evangelism—and guilty. However, Jesus simply said to look for people who want to listen to you—people you will encounter in your everyday walk.

This is something they can do within their existing contacts and relationships. There is a great burden lifted from our people as we share with them God's part in the process.

Trouble

If the teacher is not received, said Jesus, the students should not expect a warm welcome either. As we go out into the world looking for the Person of Peace and sharing the Good News of the kingdom of God, we must expect trouble in our lives. There will be many who are not yet ready to hear the message, and they will react strongly against what they perceive as intolerance or insensitivity on your part. It is not an "if" but a "when" as to this happening.

Our mission to the world has not changed. What we need now is to express it in such a way that everyone in our churches feels empowered to participate. As we look at the final seven principles in the Octagon, remember that all of the principles in the LifeShapes will help you build and equip your people for this mission.

In the inner city, we did many things to be present in our community. One regular job was to pick up litter and junk from around the apartments. These areas were really dirty and had loads of trash scattered about. During one of our clean-up days, a set of 16-year-old Asian twins called to us from their third story window asking who we were and why we were doing what we were. I perceived through the Holy Spirit that they were looking for Christ so I sent someone up to pray with them. Then and there they became Christians and they have gone on to become strong disciples of Christ.

—MIKE

Presence: Jesus Is Where You Are

Presence evangelism occurs when you are present in a situation or with an individual or group. Where you are is always an opportunity to model Jesus, acting as he would act, speaking as he would speak. As you show kindness and speak encouragement, a Person of Peace may become evident to you. Perhaps you are in a committee meeting and you speak in a positive way where others are complaining. After the meeting another committee member comes up to you and thanks you for remaining positive. This could be a Person of Peace making himself known. An opportunity to share why you are upbeat is open to you because you are present. As the wise man said, "Wherever you go, there you are." And wherever you are may be an opportunity to meet with a Person of Peace.

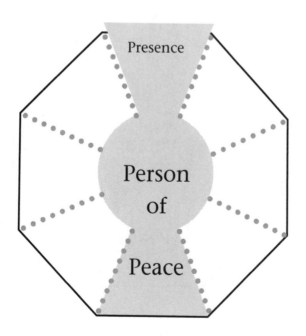

PASSING RELATIONSHIPS: THE SPIRIT

People we meet only once or twice are what we would call passing relationships. The clerk at the gas station. A stranger standing in line at the bank. The person we happen to sit next to on a plane. Most likely, even if they show themselves to be a Person of Peace at that moment, we are not going to lead them into a personal relationship with Christ in our brief encounter. But we may be used to take them closer to that point. Paul said that some plant, some water, and God gives the harvest (1 Cor. 3:6). In a passing relationship, you may be called on to plant a seed or to water what has already been planted. Just because you do not see the end result does not mean you are not a vital part of the process.

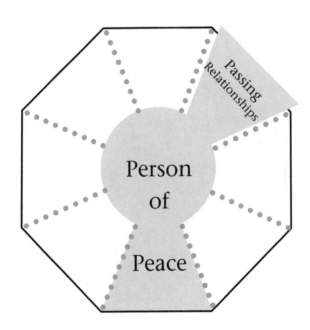

PERMANENT RELATIONSHIPS: THE MARATHON

Permanent relationships are those in your family and with close friends. If a passing relationship is like a sprint, permanent relationships are a marathon. You are with these people often, and for extended periods of time. It is important that you do not force the Gospel message when this person is not ready. You may have to wait for a long time before he or she is a Person of Peace for you, but until that time their heart is not ready to hear you. It seems we have the hardest time sharing our faith with those closest to us. Perhaps this is in part due to our impatience. We want so much for them to live in the incredible kingdom life we are experiencing that we rush them before God has prepared them to hear us. Pray, wait, and watch. God is never in a hurry, and he is never late.

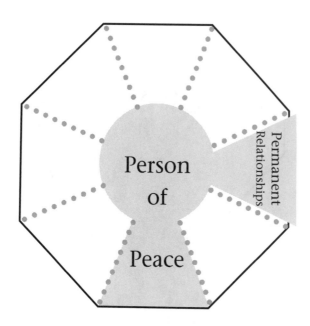

PROCLAMATION AS IDENTIFICATION

Most pastors love opportunities to proclaim the Gospel to those who are not believers. Weddings and funerals are two gatherings of nonbelievers with whom we can share a salvation message. This is fine, as long as we understand we are not going to convince those who are not ready to receive. That is not how it works. Our proclamation should be used to identify those who are Persons of Peace, then enter into relationships with them, or connect them with others who can walk with them in the initial stages of discipleship. This is what evangelism really is: inviting a person to walk the walk of faith, not just pray a prayer.

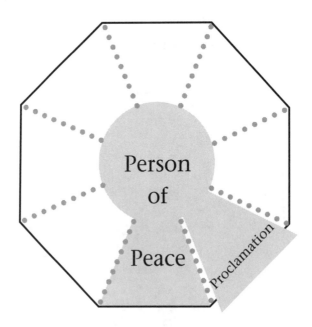

PREPARATION: MOVING PEOPLE ALONG THE SCALE

Preparation is similar to cultivating soil and planting seed in advance of the harvest. Often our words will be one turn of a person's soil. Another comes along and, sensing an opportunity with a Person of Peace, turns the soil once again. The next week, the soil gets turned over one more time. Then yet another comes and plants seed. A few more come and water the seed. None of these individual workers see what the others have done, and perhaps none will be there for the harvest. But all have had a hand in making a disciple.

Dr. James F. Engel (Wheaton Graduate School) developed a model that is helpful for those engaged in the communication of the Gospel. Known as the Engel Scale, this model gives insight into the decision-making process of the unbeliever. On this scale, a person who asks forgiveness of sin and is born again spiritually would be at the "zero" point of the scale. To the right of this point are positive numbers— +1, +3, +5, etc. As the disciple grows and

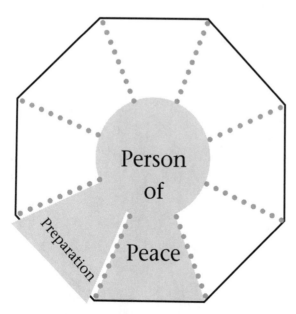

matures in his walk, he progresses to the right of the scale.[20]

To the left of zero are corresponding negative numbers. A person who is open to listening to your experiences with God and is asking questions about the kingdom could be said to be a -1. This is a Person of Peace. Someone who is not interested at this time in spiritual matters could be a -5. And the one who would rather knock your teeth down your throat than hear about Christ is a -10. If, in the preparation phase of the Octagon, you move a person from -5 to -3, is this not evangelism? We may not be there for the "zero hour," but we will have been used by God in the process.

POWER: AWE AS EVANGELISM

Jesus often used demonstrations of the power of God to identify the Person of Peace. Praying for the sick and seeing a miraculous healing will often reveal a Person of Peace, whether the one prayed for or simply one

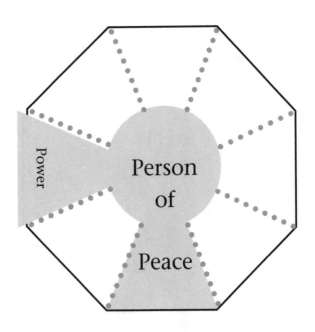

watching. Our God is, truly, an awesome God. He will do things to create awe in those who have yet to commit their hearts to him. We do not create these miracles, nor can we box God up and manipulate when and where miracles will occur. All we can do is be ready when they do happen. The Person of Peace for our life may be revealed at that moment, and we should be ready for this time.

PERCEPTION: FEELING THE TEMPERATURE

Perception is what Peter Wagner called "testing the soil." We need to be spiritually perceptive to situations and circumstances, as well as to individuals, in order to identify the Person of Peace. For instance, in a presence evangelism setting, you are golfing with three other men you just met on the first tee. As you complete your round and are shaking hands after the eighteenth hole, ask yourself, "What was the temperature of the soil?

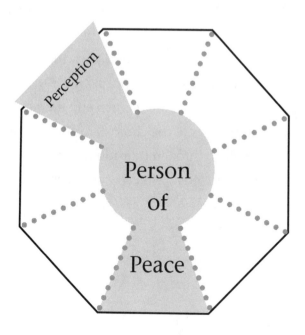

Was it hot, warm, or cold?" If the temperature was cold—none of the men exhibited any signs of being open to you sharing the Good News with them—move on. Shake the dust from your cleats, as it were, and wish them well. But if you sense any warmth in the soil, pursue a further relationship with that person. He is a Person of Peace for you.

The eight principles of the Octagon provide a comprehensive but not exhaustive approach to evangelism that, along with the other LifeShapes, have proven to be effective for the church transitioning from the old maps to a new way of reaching today's postmodern culture. God is doing a new thing in our land and in our churches and we want to perceive and participate in it. Being aware of God's ways and work can help God's people meet the challenge of our day. God promises that he will build his church and the gates of hell will not prevail against it. The best days of the church are ahead of us. Even though every existing church will go through transitions, we can be brave, be bold, and believe that what we do today will echo in eternity.

> Our mission at Community Church of Joy is "That all may have a personal relationship with Jesus Christ and become empowered followers, we share His love, with joy, inspired by the Holy Spirit." The purpose of our community is to be intentional about being Jesus to the lost. Those searching for spiritual connection are different today than they were even a decade ago. They want to experience God and encounter his powerful presence. These eight principles are helping us to fulfill our mission.
>
> —WALT

CHAPTER 24

CONCLUSION

We began this book with a trip back in history to look at cultural earthquakes, how they changed the course of those living at the time, and how the current quake is affecting the effectiveness of today's church. As church leaders, we are uniquely positioned to point our people back to the Compass—to lead the church through this time of transition into a better place, a place of renewed passion and purpose.

There will always be seasons of cultural upheaval. When the mighty Roman Empire fell, the shock waves from that quake circled the globe. In the British Isles, the aftereffect on the church was astounding. Even as the Romans were withdrawing, the Christian faith was growing in both Britain and Ireland. The Celts were great missionaries, spreading the Gospel back into Europe and founding churches and monasteries wherever they went. In doing so, these Celtic Christians reclaimed former pagan temples and buildings that had been abandoned by the Romans and began using them for God.

The Celtic church continued to grow in the aftershocks of tremendous cultural upheaval. They began to build new faith communities amidst the ruins of Roman architectural sites. At some sites, an archway may have been all that remained as testament to the former glory of Rome. The Celts built around this arch, making it the doorway or a window for a new building that would house those who glorified God. A solitary column left standing became an interior support and scattered stones were gathered together to form a foundation or wall to house a church. In this way, the Celts made good use of what had lasted the test of time while building something for the time they were in.

In the same way, the transitional church—the church that is bridging this time between modernity and postmodernity—is not to abandon all that has gone before. We need to understand the value of the old ways while embracing the new. We need to use all the materials that God has given us towards one goal—the expansion of his kingdom on earth. We may need to throw out our maps but our Compass can point us to what is true.

THE NEXT STEP

In the short time of applying Lifeshapes at Community Church of Joy, I have had numerous people tell me that most things have changed, and they like it! Joy has stopped doing church and is learning how to be the church. As a staff and as a congregation, we are experiencing a rebirth of passion in our lives and in our church. Soon, my utmost prayer that our whole community will be transformed will become a reality. Wow! For Christ's sake, may it be so.

—*WALT*

Discipleship Jesus' way is not just another way to live, it's the only way to live. What has been presented in this book honestly works—we've witnessed it's success throughout England, across America, and in other faith communities around the world. It works because it is not a program for doing but rather a process of being. When these shapes get into the DNA of a believer, it is truly remarkable what God can do.

These principles can give your church a new understanding of how to build an authentic community whose mission is to advance the kingdom of God. Worship can become a bigger part of daily life instead of just a weekend experience. You can discover how to confidently release ministry into the hands of the whole population of believers so that the priesthood of believers is more than an ideology—it's a practice. All God's people living as empowered, equipped, and employed ministers and missionaries will do a much better job of advancing the kingdom than just us few trained professionals.

> YOU CAN DISCOVER HOW TO CONFIDENTLY RELEASE MINISTRY INTO THE HANDS OF THE WHOLE POPULATION OF BELIEVERS SO THAT THE PRIESTHOOD OF BELIEVERS IS MORE THAN AN IDEOLOGY—IT'S A PRACTICE.

Here's how to use this book: read it; pray about it; teach concepts from it to your staff, your congregation, your family; evaluate the impact and then begin again. Read more; pray more; teach more; and evaluate more. Don't stop. Learning how to live as Jesus lived and love as Jesus loved will bring amazing fresh passion to your church. And we are convinced that discovering how to learn as Jesus learned and leading as Jesus led will produce greater faithfulness and fruitfulness for you and for every believer in the corner of the world God has given to you.

For more resources on LifeShapes, visit www.LifeShapes.com or contact your local Christian bookstore.

APPENDIX

Fivefold Ministries Questionnaire

Read through the statements and decide as honestly as you can whether they apply to you often, sometimes, or rarely, and check the appropriate box. Do not linger on each item, as your first throught is likely to represent the most accurate response.

Item no.		Often	Some-times	Rarely
1	I remember names or at least where I first met someone			
2	I have expressed my feelings about God as pictures or analogies			
3	My ability to present Scripture clearly and accurately has been commented on			
4	I can be counted on to contribute original ideas			
5	I find myself talking about my faith to the people I meet			
6	I get frustrated when I feel I'm not experiencing "new" things as a Christian			
7	When I communicate biblical truths to others I see resulting changes in knowledge, attitudes, values, or conduct			
8	I share what knowledge I have with others			
9	I have an urge to share thoughts with people that I felt when I prayed, and I have been told they meant something or were relevant to the person's current situation			
10	I get upset at other people's difficulties and problems even if I haven't experienced them myself			
11	I have a strong sense of what God wants to say to people in response to a particular situation			
12	I enjoy studying the Scriptures and find that I get fresh insights that people find interesting and helpful			
13	When reading the Bible I am more able to grasp the wider picture or message than the specific details			
14	I like to share what I believe			
15	I have been successful in developing Christian discipline in others			
16	I'll try things out if it will encourage others to do the same			

Item no.		Often	Some-times	Rarely
17	I am quick to help when help is needed and often do things that I see need to be done without even being asked			
18	I have been able to spot a "person of peace" who is ready to receive a word from God and have seen a positive response			
19	I have a clear vision and others have said that they feel confident to go along with me			
20	I try explaining things in different ways if people are finding a concept difficult to grasp or understand			
21	I think before I speak			
22	I really fear that people I know will not be saved			
23	I like to be clear and decisive when speaking about what I believe God has said to me			
24	I am by no means an expert on Scripture, but I can grasp the point of a passage quite quickly			
25	I get frustrated and even depressed at the lack of faith or understanding of others around me			
26	People tell me that the things I say often help them to try new things for God			
27	I am interested in living and working overseas or among people from a different culture			
28	I am good at listening and taking in what people say			
29	I have contrived situations so that non-Christians are prompted to ask spiritual questions			
30	I have helped fellow believers by guiding them to relevant portions of the Bible			
31	I get excited when I discover new understanding, insights, and applications of God's Word			
32	I have reminded people of the foundations of their faith			
33	Despite not enjoying the nitty-gritty details of leadership, I still often end up leading things			
34	People have told me that I have helped them be restored to the Christian community			
35	I feel that I know exactly what God wants to do in ministry at a specific point in time			
36	I dig out information and passages to explain a concept			
37	I mix easily with a wide variety of people without having to try to be one of them			

Item no.		Often	Some-times	Rarely
38	I have a deep concern to encourage people toward spiritual growth and achievement			
39	I try to think of different ways of expressing the truth of the Gospel			
40	Friends ask me to help clarify a situation or Scripture			
41	I am quite persuasive when encouraging people to examine their spiritual motives			
42	I empathize with those who are hurting or broken and can support them through their pain to wholeness			
43	When in a group, I am the one others often look to for vision and direction			
44	I enjoy being with nonbelievers because of my desire to win them to Christ			
45	I will see a job through to the end so that no one has to pick up the pieces after me			
46	My prayers surprise me with their clarity and unexpected direction			
47	People comment that they remember what I tell them about God			
48	I expect opportunities for witnessing to arise rather than react in surprise when they occur			
49	I desire the gift of healing in greater measure (that the Lord would heal others through me)			
50	The things I say in a spiritual context make people feel uncomfortable			
51	I have enjoyed relating to a certain group of people over a period of time, sharing personally in their successes and their failures			
52	People have told me that I have helped them learn biblical truth in a meaningful way			
53	I have led someone to a decision for salvation through faith in Christ			
54	God has enabled me to reveal specific things that have happened or meant something at a later date			
55	There have been times when I felt sure I knew God's specific will for the future growth of his work, even when others have not been so sure			
56	People have told me that I have communicated timely words or pictures that must have come directly from the Lord			
57	People call on me to help those who are less fortunate			
58	I get great satisfaction from studying the Bible and sharing my insights with others			
59	Others have suggested that I am a person of unusual vision			

Item no.		Often	Some-times	Rarely
60	Non-Christians have noted that they feel comfortable when they are around me, and that I have a positive effect on them toward developing a faith in Christ			
61	I am willing to challenge or confront people in order to help them mature			
62	I regularly need to get space alone or long periods of time out to reflect, pray, and think			
63	I have just suddenly known something about someone			
64	I enjoy taking notes when someone is speaking and pay close attention to the details of what they are saying			
65	I am faithful in providing support, care, and nurture for others over long periods of time, even when others have stopped			
66	I enjoy mentoring individuals			
67	I enjoy relating stories and sharing my experiences			
68	I enjoy coming up with new and original ideas, dreaming big, and thinking about vision for the future			
69	I find non-Christians ask me questions about my faith in Christ and my church involvement			
70	I can accurately assess a person based on first impressions and know instinctively when something is not quite right			
71	I like to provide a safe and comfortable environment where people feel they are welcome, that they belong, are listened to, and cared for			
72	I would like to start a church or a new ministry in an area that is not catered for at present			
73	I have a heart to share my faith and to pray for those in my work and neighborhood who do not attend church			
74	When I hear about situations of need I feel burdened to pray			
75	I like to help churches, organizations, groups, and leaders become more efficient and often find myself thinking about how things function			
76	I enjoy spending time studying Scripture and prefer to do so systematically			
77	I look for opportunities to socialize and build relationship with non-Christians			
78	People come to me to ask my opinions on particular parts of the Bible or to answer their queries			

Item no.		Often	Some-times	Rarely
79	I find that people trust me and come to me regularly wanting to chat and looking for my advice, prayers, and help			
80	I can clarify goals, develop strategies, and use resources effectively to accomplish tasks			

FIVEFOLD MINISTRY SCORE SHEET

- Place a check for each item number for which you answered "often" or "sometimes." (The "rarely" answers are not counted but you may wish to use the shaded column for "rarely" so as to keep tabs on which answers you have transferred from the question sheet.)
- Note that some questions occur more than once in the columns below.
- Finally, add up the number of "often" checks, double the answer, and add to the number of checks for "sometimes."

FIVEFOLD MINISTRY SCORE SHEET

Item no.	Often	Sometimes	Rarely	Item no.	Often	Sometimes	Rarely	Item no.	Often	Sometimes	Rarely	Item no.	Often	Sometimes	Rarely	Item no.	Often	Sometimes	Rarely	
1				2				3				5				4				
10				9				7				14				6				
17				11				8				18				13				
21				23				12				22				16				
28				25				15				29				19				
30				31				20				32				26				
34				35				24				37				27				
42				41				36				39				33				
45				46				40				44				38				
49				50				47				48				43				
51				54				52				53				55				
57				56				58				60				59				
53				27				21				1				32				
60				55				39				51				11				
65				62				64				61				68				
66				63				67				69				72				
71				70				76				73				75				
79				74				78				77				80				

Total of items marked "often"	Total of items marked "often"	Total of items marked "often"	Total of items marked "often"	Total of items marked "often"
Multiply by 2	Multiply by 2	Multiply by 2	Multiply by 2	Multiply by 2
Total of items marked "sometimes"	Total of items marked "sometimes"	Total of items marked "sometimes"	Total of items marked "sometimes"	Total of items marked "sometimes"
Grand Total	Grand Total	Grand Total	Grand Total	Grand Total
PASTOR	**PROPHET**	**TEACHER**	**EVANGELIST**	**APOSTLE**

Endnotes

1. The Barna Update, "Number of Unchurched Adults Has Nearly Doubled Since 1991," May 4, 2004, www.barna.org.

2. Dr. Eddie Gibbs, e-mail message to author, August 2, 2004.

3. John Piper, Brothers, *We Are Not Professionals: A Plea to Pastors for Radical Ministry* (Nashville: Broadman and Holman, 2002), 1.

4. Ibid., 2.

5. Larry Crabb, *The Safest Place on Earth* (Nashville, TN: W Publishing Group, 1999), 30-31.

6. Health Expressions™, "Work-Related Stress," 2004, www.healthexpressions.com/stress_busters/index.shtml.

7. *Secondhand Lions*. Screenplay by Tim McCanlies. Dir. Tim McCanlies. Perf. Michael Caine and Robert Duvall. New Line Cinema, 2003.

8. Brother Lawrence and Frank Laubach, *Practicing His Presence* (Goleta, CA: Christian Books, 1973), 44.

9. A. W. Tozer,*The Pursuit of God* (Harrisonburg, PA: Christians Publications, Inc., 1948), 34.

10. Donald Miller, *Blue Like Jazz* (Nelson, 2003), 233.

11. Craig Detweiler and Barry Taylor, A *Matrix of Meanings: Finding God in Pop Culture* (Grand Rapids, MI: Baker Academic, 2003), 81.

12. Danny Wallace, *The Joy of Sects: The Join Me Story,* Join Me, www.join-me.co.uk/story.html.

13. Check out Ken Blanchard's new material at www.leadlikejesus.com.

14. Dan Kimball, *The Emerging Church* (Grand Rapids, MI: Zondervan, 2003), 248.

15. Piper, Brothers, *We Are Not Professionals*, 11.

16. Kimball, *The Emerging Church*, 92.

17. Andrew Murray, *With Christ in the School of Prayer* (Old Tappan, NJ: Fleming H. Revell Company, 1984), 16.

18. Mike White, "Clinical Studies about the Importance of Optimal Breathing." *Optimal Breathing*®: www.breathing.com (November 19, 2004).

19. Oswald Chambers, *My Utmost for His Highest* (New Jersey: Barbour and Company, Inc., 1935) 342.

20. Michael L. Simpson, *Permission Evangelism* (Colorado Springs, CO: Cook Communications Ministries 2003), 51.

21. *An Interpersonal Communication Model: The Engel Scale Explained,* November 19, 2004, www.gospelcom.net/guide/resources/tellitoften.php.

Turn the page for a sneak peek into the next book on LifeShapes...

A
PASSIONATE
LIFE

Believers yearn to have an intimate relationship with Jesus and authentic, loving community with each other. They long to live in a way that leaves a significant impact on their world. To all who follow his teachings, Jesus promises a full life, *A Passionate Life*.

By learning and practicing the principles represented in the same eight shapes introduced in *The Passionate Church*, believers begin to live as Jesus taught his disciples to live . . . simply, purposefully, passionately.

Available May 2005

THE SUN SHOWER

*E*xactly what is this passionate life Jesus is calling you to and why do you sometimes feel that everyone else gets it but you? Exodus 34:14 (NLT) tells us that our God "is passionate about his relationship with you." As a Jesus follower, it is only natural that your heart respond to him in kind, so what's missing? Here's a story from Mike that illustrates what we're talking about:

While living in Sheffield, England, my family and I joined a health club. My wife, Sally, and our three children—Rebecca, Elizabeth, and Sam—enjoyed all the typical instruments of torture like weights and treadmills, plus a pool and hot tub. One week I was relaxing in the hot tub when my daughters came up to me and asked if I had tried the Sun Shower yet.

"I don't even know what a Sun Shower is," I said. "What is it?"

"It's that white tube over by the pool. You stand up in it and get a tan, but you also get totally refreshed. It's like standing on the beach in South Carolina."

Now, as far as the Breen family is concerned, the beaches of South Carolina are the closest things to perfection that you can find here on earth. I agreed to give it a try.

"What does it take?" I asked. They said it was a pound for three minutes. So I took a one-pound coin and walked over to the Sun Shower. The door opened to a room the size of a small closet. I walked in, closed the door, and read the instructions clear through. I put on a pair of goggles that was hanging in there and shut my eyes tightly. Doing this, of course, meant I couldn't see to insert the coin. So I opened my eyes, took off the goggles, put the coin in the slot, pulled the goggles back on, and waited.

Nothing.

Well, I heard a slight whirring sound and a few clicks, but I felt nothing. When the three minutes were up, the whirring stopped and I stepped out.

"What did you think?" my daughters asked. They were so excited for me to experience what they obviously thought was a fantastic idea that I was sorry to have to let them down.

"Well," I said, "I guess I just don't get it. I mean, it was okay, but probably something you girls would like better."

They were profoundly disappointed that I hadn't shared their experience. I thought the whole thing was rather strange, but I didn't say much about it.

The next week Rebecca and Elizabeth came up to me again at the gym.

"Dad, this time try it for six minutes. Maybe three minutes wasn't enough for you to start feeling the effects. Give it six minutes, okay?"

SIX MINUTES IS A LONG TIME TO WAIT WHEN YOU'RE STANDING IN AN ENCLOSED BOOTH WITH YOUR EYES SHUT, LISTENING TO WHIRRING AND CLICKING NOISES.

I started to tell them how silly the whole thing was, but they were giving me such looks that no father could say "No." So back I went to the white tube. I stepped inside the room, pulled the door closed, read the instructions, put on the goggles, pulled the goggles off, slipped two pounds into the coin slot, put the goggles back on, and waited.

Six minutes is a long time to wait when you're standing in an enclosed booth with your eyes shut, listening to whirring and clicking noises. When it was over, I took off the goggles and hung them back on the hook and left.

"How was it this time, Dad? Did you feel the effects this time?"

They thought I was daft when I said I really didn't think it was for me. "This is something for you and your friends to enjoy," I said. "Maybe I'm just too old to get the full benefits of it." They were disappointed again, but one thing I must say for my children: they don't give up easily.

The next week they were ready.

"Dad, try it this time for nine minutes. You'll really love it if you give it enough time. Nine minutes should do it for you. C'mon, Dad!"

I looked over at Sally for support, but she just gave me the "You got yourself into this, get yourself out" look. So off I went for the third time to the Sun Shower.

I went in the tube, pulled the door shut, read the instructions clear through (for the third time—they hadn't changed), put on the goggles, took the goggles off to put in three pounds, put the goggles back on, and closed my eyes.

> I TURNED THE KNOB, AND THE DOOR OPENED TO A ROOM FILLED WITH THE MOST REFRESHING LIGHT RAYS AND REPLICATED OCEAN BREEZE I COULD EVER IMAGINE.

Let me tell you, nine minutes is a long time to stand in a closet in the dark listening to clicks and whirrs. So I took a chance and opened my eyes—only to find that I could see right through the goggles. Looking around, I wondered if I would get more of a tan standing closer to the mirror. Then I saw some things that looked like coat hooks on the wall, and thought that maybe they were there to reflect the rays. Turning around, I saw a doorknob. What was this? I turned the knob, and the door opened to a room filled with the most refreshing light rays and replicated ocean breeze I could ever imagine.

I had been standing for three weeks in the changing room.

All this time I thought I was having the experience I was supposed to have. I had tried to work up feelings of refreshment, but I knew that they weren't real. As hard as I tried, I just didn't get it!

Is your experience with Jesus like this? Have you been standing in the changing room for weeks and months, even years, wondering what's so great about being a Christian? You see others at church or in your small group, and they talk about how wonderful it is to know Jesus, really know him like you can your best friend, and you long for that same experience. Maybe you even try to put on a good show, telling your friends how much Jesus means to you even though it's not true.

> MAYBE YOU EVEN TRY TO PUT ON A GOOD SHOW, TELLING YOUR FRIENDS HOW MUCH JESUS MEANS TO YOU EVEN THOUGH IT'S NOT TRUE.

Perhaps you attend church every week but come away feeling empty, thinking it's a great waste of time. Yet others come out refreshed, so you keep going back, putting your money in the coin slot and telling your friends what an exhilarating feeling you have, too. But you know it isn't working for you.

Jesus would not have invited us to be his friends if he didn't mean it. He would not have called us to follow him if we were not meant to see where he is going. This is what we're inviting you to do: walk with Jesus. It sounds simple, doesn't

We're not here to give you another list of things you are doing wrong, or a set of guidelines to follow each day so you can fake the feeling some more. This is not Eight Secrets to a Better Life. We've been where you are. We were tired of faking our relationship with Jesus. We wanted it to be real. We wanted it to be passionate. And it is.

— MIKE & WALT

it? It is simple but it's not easy. We can help you develop a deeper understanding of what it means to walk with Jesus—to be his follower, his disciple—in a way that you can remember and apply to every situation and relationship in your life.

So what are you waiting for? Come on—open the door. Leave the closet of spiritual emptiness and step into the light of a passionate Christian life!

The Word at Work . . .

What would you do if you wanted to share God's love with children on the streets of your city? That's the dilemma David C. Cook faced in 1870s Chicago. His answer was to create literature that would capture children's hearts.

Out of those humble beginnings grew a worldwide ministry that has used literature to proclaim God's love and disciple generation after generation. Cook Communications Ministries is committed to personal discipleship—to helping people of all ages learn God's Word, embrace his salvation, walk in his ways, and minister in his name.

Opportunities—and Crisis

We live in a land of plenty—including plenty of Christian literature! But what about the rest of the world? Jesus commanded, "Go and make disciples of all nations" (Matt. 28:19) and we want to obey this commandment. But how does a publishing organization "go" into all the world?

There are five times as many Christians around the world as there are in North America. Christian workers in many of these countries have no more than a New Testament, or perhaps a single shared copy of the Bible, from which to learn and teach.

We are committed to sharing what God has given us with such Christians.

A vital part of Cook Communications Ministries is our international outreach, Cook Communications Ministries International (CCMI). Your purchase of this book, and of other books and Christian-growth products from Cook, enables CCMI to provide Bibles and Christian literature to people in more than 150 languages in 65 countries.

Cook Communications Ministries is a not-for-profit, self-supporting organization. Revenues from sales of our books, Bible curricula, and other church and home products not only fund our U.S. ministry, but also fund our CCMI ministry around the world. One hundred percent of donations to CCMI go to our international literature programs.

. . . Around the World

CCMI reaches out internationally in three ways:

· Our premier International Christian Publishing Institute (ICPI) trains leaders from nationally led publishing houses around the world to develop evangelism and discipleship materials to transform lives in their countries.

· We provide literature for pastors, evangelists, and Christian workers in their national language. We provide study helps for pastors and lay leaders in many parts of the world, such as China, India, Cuba, Iran, and Vietnam.

· We reach people at risk—refugees, AIDS victims, street children, and famine victims—with God's Word. CCMI puts literature that shares the Good News into the hands of people at spiritual risk—people who might die before they hear the name of Jesus and are transformed by his love.

Word Power, God's Power

Faith Kidz, RiverOak, Honor, Life Journey, Victor, NexGen — every time you purchase a book produced by Cook Communications Ministries, you not only meet a vital personal need in your life or in the life of someone you love, but you're also a part of ministering to José in Colombia, Humberto in Chile, Gousa in India, or Lidiane in Brazil. You help make it possible for a pastor in China, a child in Peru, or a mother in West Africa to enjoy a life-changing book. And because you helped, children and adults around the world are learning God's Word and walking in his ways.

Thank you for your partnership in helping to disciple the world. May God bless you with the power of his Word in your life.

For more information about our
international ministries, visit www.ccmi.org.

LIFESHAPES

Building a generation of *passionate* believers

Join the LifeShapes community — check us out online at: www.lifeshapes.com

- View sample chapters of future LifeShapes publications — before you can buy them in the stores!

- Post your thoughts/experiences on our bulletin board

- Connect with others whose lives are being changed through the LifeShapes movement!

- Download LifeShapes streaming audio & video featuring authors Michael Breen & Walt Kallestad

- Sign up for future online training events with LifeShapes trainers

- Feed your passion: Subscribe to the monthly LifeShapes e-newsletter

And much more!

We can't wait to see you online! Log on today!

LIFESHAPES.COM